The Art of

Chinese

Vegetarian Cooking

Also in the Series

The Art of Japanese Vegetarian Cooking

Coming Soon

The Art of Mediterranean Vegetarian Cooking
The Art of Italian Vegetarian Cooking

The Art of

Chinese

Vegetarian Cooking

JOANNE HUSH

WITH

PAUL HUSH

PRIMA PUBLISHING

PRIMA PUBLISHING and colophon are trademarks of Prima Communications, Inc.

Illustrations by Jaime Robles

Library of Congress Cataloging-in-Publication Data

Hush, Joanne.
   The art of Chinese vegetarian cooking / by Joanne with Paul Hush.
     p.   cm.—(The art of vegetarian cooking)
   Includes index.
   ISBN 0-7615-0434-6
   1. Vegetarian cookery. 2. Cookery, Chinese. I. Hush, Paul. II. Title. III. Series.
TX837.H875   1996
641.5'636'0951—dc20   96-229
                                        CIP

96 97 98 99 00 AA 10 9 8 7 6 5 4 3 2 1

Printed in the United States of America

HOW TO ORDER

Single copies may be ordered from Prima Publishing, P.O. Box 1260BK, Rocklin, CA 95677; telephone (916) 632-4400. Quantity discounts are also available. On your letterhead include information concerning the intended use of the books and the number of books you wish to purchase.

Table of Contents

Preface

Some who pick up this book are year-round vegetarians. Others eat meat only occasionally, and still others are just looking for something new and different to add to their cooking repertoire. We welcome all of you to Chinese vegetarian cooking.

Vegetarian Times magazine counts more than 12.5 million full- or part-time vegetarians in the U.S., twice as many as ten years ago. Interest in meatless diets continues to grow, particularly among young people. Philosophical beliefs are a reason for this growth, but, according to *Vegetarian Times*, it mostly has to do with health concerns. The latest federal dietary guidelines confirm that we all should be eating more grains, vegetables, and fruit, and less meat.

Americans, and most Europeans, eat too much fat. This is a major cause of excess weight and a contributor to heart problems, cancer, diabetes, and other health risks, according to most health professionals. Avoiding meat eliminates the main source of fat in the average American diet. Chinese vegetarians go even further by rarely using dairy products, which are the second major source of dietary fat.

Most vegetarians know the importance of a balanced diet, with proper nutrients from all the food groups and a healthful combination of the complex carbohydrates and proteins found in grains, beans, vegetables, and fruits. Chinese vegetarians have been following such a diet for centuries.

Chinese vegetarians have a particular advantage. They have the long-time traditions of Chinese cooking and the many herbs and spices and marinades and sauces that make their food so appealing. And the Chinese have a knack for bringing together appetizing combinations of flavors. Spicy and savory, sweet and sour meld to create meatless cuisine that is never bland.

The Chinese have another quality that relates to food. It is a real caring about the look and significance of everyday things. Many foods have symbolic meanings in China and special attention is given to the presentation of food, as well as to the nuances of its taste. There is indeed an art to Chinese vegetarian cooking, and we hope you will enjoy it.

Acknowledgments

We wish to give special thanks to our friend Ginger Shaffer for her computer skills and invaluable help in the preparation of this manuscript and to our editor at Prima Publishing, Betsy Towner, for her good ideas and friendly spirit.

A Cuisine for the Ages

*I*T SEEMED THAT WE had stepped into the wonderland of a Chinese silk painting. It was 1981 in Beijing, soon after China's reopening to foreign visitors after years of national turmoil and isolation. As cookbook writers, we were invited to a special banquet at the Fang Shan Restaurant on the grounds of the Imperial Palace, once the home of emperors—now a place for tourists.

The Fang Shan Restaurant sits on a tiny island in a small, bright blue, jewel of a lake, surrounded by carefully tended lawns. The building was classically Chinese with a pagoda-style roof and red wooden trim. In the quiet interior it was easy to imagine that there in the alcove is where the emperor and his party must have sat.

The menu at the Fang Shan was a re-creation of a court banquet. It was immediately clear that the emperors must have been a very adventurous eaters, dining on such exotic delicacies as duck foot webbing and black bear paws. There were ministers of cuisine in the courts of China before most of the rest of the world knew of gourmet food, and these chefs must have been allowed to let their imaginations take flight.

We soon learned that the Fang Shan was one of a kind. As our tour made its way around China that year, we found that almost no restaurants were open to visitors. Tourists were expected to eat as a group at the hotels. We did manage to get out to restaurants on our own in Shanghai and Guangzhou, and to talk with chefs in the Beijing Hotel and elsewhere, but our hopes to make this trip a food tour of China were only partially fulfilled.

At the time, apparently, very few restaurants in China were considered prestigious enough to serve foreign visitors. It seemed that during the dark years of the cultural revolution many of the great restaurants of China, with their classic traditions of haute cuisine, were no longer wanted. The China of the 1960s and 1970s had no place for such frivolities. Even in China it was acknowledged that one had to go to Hong Kong to find great Chinese food.

WAITING FOR BETTER DAYS

Through these hard times, the Chinese people's indomitable spirit helped them survive, as it has historically through times of war and famine, and as it will continue to do through whatever troubles may lie ahead.

Chinese food traditions, too, persevere. A new generation of chefs has now come along in China to carry on the techniques, sauces, and food presentation that can be traced back for thousands of years. In the last fifteen years, as tourism has been encouraged in China, many new hotels and restaurants have begun again to celebrate the grand traditions of Chinese cooking. These traditions were never lost or forgotten, just left simmering to wait for better days.

But the history of food in China has been molded by the history of its troubles. The emperors may have been concerned with high cuisine, but the people worried about rice and vegetables. As floods, droughts, and wars wiped out harvests, the people had to manage as best they could with whatever ingredients they could bring together.

This very hardship has lent to an incredible variety of vegetarian possibilities for the Chinese table. There is probably no part of any plant that is known in China that has not appeared on a dinner table in one form or another, at one time or another. And in China, "a full bowl of rice" symbolizes a person's well-being, and the greeting "Have you had your rice today?" is a common way of saying "How are you?"

PHILOSOPHIC INFLUENCES

Chinese food has certainly been affected, too, by the great philosophic and religious movements in China—Confucianism, Buddhism, and Taoism. Each of these speaks of a fundamental harmony of man and nature, and this is reflected in the many ways of Chinese life. The harmonious melding of opposing forces, of yin and yang, is very much a part of Chinese cuisine—sweet and sour, hot and bland, crunchy and smooth.

Buddhism has had perhaps the greatest influence on vegetarian cooking in particular. Buddhists believe that all creatures are sacred and none should be killed unnecessarily. Not all Buddhists are full-time vegetarians, but their beliefs form a philosophical base for vegetarianism that is widely accepted around the world.

Chinese cooking is tradition married to innovation. Thousands of years of history make room for constant experimentation with new ideas and new ingredients. Already there seems to be more variety in Chinese cooking than in any other cuisine. And by Chinese standards, we have hardly begun.

The Art of

Chinese

Vegetarian Cooking

The Chinese Vegetarian

In China, vegetarianism has drawn nourishment from religious ideas and cultural traditions throughout its history. Over this time, many millions of Chinese—from Buddhist monks to country housewives, literary scholars to restaurant chefs—have helped to find thousands of appetizing and ingenious ways to prepare and serve vegetables. We are all the beneficiaries of this culinary evolution.

The Chinese cuisine begins with rice (in the south) and wheat (in the north), which is the fiber and the complex carbohydrate that nutritionists tell us is essential to a healthful diet. The Chinese have known this all along. Noodles and other pastas are an important part of the Chinese diet, too—adding more complex carbohydrates. Nutritionists tell us that we should eat more beans and legumes as a source of protein, along with grains, and the Chinese have been doing this for generations. The Chinese, and the Japanese, have transformed the simple soybean into an important flavoring ingredient (soy and other sauces) and a major protein source (bean curd/tofu) now used around the world. Nutritionists also tell us we should base our diet on vegetables and fruit, and again the Chinese have shown the way.

The cooking methods favored by the Chinese—stir-frying and steaming—are particularly well suited to cooking vegetables. Stir-frying heats foods for only the briefest time needed to cook them through and to blend the ingredients together. This quick cooking at high heat helps to retain the natural flavors and nutrients in foods. Steaming, too, is a quick and nutritionally sound way of cooking vegetables, and it has the added value of helping to keep them moist and tender.

In our Chinese cooking, and so in the recipes in this book, we make one departure from traditional practices. In the interest of good nutrition, we use much less cooking oil (and less sodium too) than you'll find in most Chinese recipes. Vegetarian cooking is by its nature a healthful way of eating and should be as low in fat as possible.

To reduce the amount of fat in stir-frying, we use a nonstick wok rather than a standard carbon steel wok. This enables us to cook with only one or two teaspoons of oil instead of the two or three tablespoons that are usual in Chinese recipes. This cuts back the fat from cooking oil in an average recipe from forty grams (for three tablespoons of oil) to nine grams (for two teaspoons of oil). And we use canola oil, which has much less saturated fat than the peanut oil usually suggested for Chinese recipes.

We also have pretty well cut out deep-frying. Many Chinese restaurants do quite a lot of deep-frying and that's why Chinese food has been getting a reputation for being high in fat. You can't get lowfat food out of a pot filled with oil. So we choose to concentrate on the many wonderful Chinese foods that are not cooked this way. We have included a few favorite deep-fry recipes, mainly among the appetizers, which you can try if your overall fat budget is looking good that day. Otherwise, just skip those recipes. There are plenty of others to choose from.

The Chinese vegetarian uses all the special ingredients that are part of Chinese cuisine: garlic; ginger; hot and sweet peppers; scallions; Chinese herbs and spices; special sauces such as hoisin, soy, sesame, and black bean; rice vinegar; hot-and-sour combinations; traditional Chinese foods such as bean sprouts, water chestnuts, straw mushrooms, dried Chinese mushrooms, baby corn, and wontons. All of these find their way into this book. The Chinese like to bring together surprising combinations of flavors, colors, and textures, and you'll find those in this book, too.

Chinese
Cooking
Methods and
Equipment

*I*F YOU ARE NOT already cooking Chinese-style, here is all you'll need to know to get started. It's really quite easy.

THE WOK

The most important Chinese cooking method is stir-frying. You can stir-fry with a large frying pan but it's better to use a wok. The shape of the wok distributes heat more evenly and makes it easier to do the continuous stirring and tossing of ingredients that are necessary in stir-frying.

Whether you use a frying pan or a wok, we recommend that you use a non-stick pan. This cuts down on the amount of cooking oil needed, and thus reduces the fat. The recipes in this book were tested using a nonstick wok. We use one to two *teaspoons* of oil for stir-frying. If, instead, you are using a traditional carbon steel wok, you will need to use two to three *tablespoons* of cooking oil— four or five times as much.

We use a Danish-made titanium nonstick wok, brand-named Scanpan. This pan's construction incorporates the nonstick material into the metal itself, not just coating it on the surface. The result is a heavy-duty pan that holds up especially well under the high heat of stir-frying. It can be scoured with an abrasive sponge when necessary. The pan will discolor somewhat with heavy use, as does any wok, but it works far better for stir-frying than any other pan we have tried.

However, the Scanpan wok is moderately expensive, so you may prefer to try one of the other nonstick woks on the market. With careful use, another wok should do well for you, too. You may have to use a little more cooking oil than we call for, and be sure to follow the manufacturer's care and cleaning instructions.

Woks come in different sizes and have either a rounded or flattened bottom. If you have a small family, a twelve-inch-diameter wok should be adequate, but we prefer a fourteen-inch wok because it is more versatile. If you have a gas stove, it's better to use a round-bottomed wok. For an electric stove, the flat-bottomed wok is best.

CHOPPING AND DICING

Wielding the knife is the complicated part of Chinese cooking. The ingredients have to be cut up in the ways specified in the recipe or stir-frying just won't work as intended. The preparation will take a little time, but if you prepare just one Chinese recipe per meal and fill in your menu with rice or a salad or easy side dishes, you should manage quite easily.

The recipes give specific detail on the size and shape for cutting each ingredient. If the ingredients are to be cut in cubes, the recipe will tell you what size. Dicing is cutting into very small cubes. Shredding means cutting into very thin matchstick-sized pieces, and mincing is very fine chopping. Generally, all the ingredients for any given recipe will be cut to the same approximate size. This is to enable them to cook equally in the times allotted and to blend nicely together in the final presentation of the dish.

For chopping ingredients, use either a small Chinese or Japanese cleaver or a good, sharp chef's knife.

STIR-FRYING

Stir-frying is just quick cooking at high temperatures. We give specific instructions in each recipe, but basically all that's required is first to heat the wok over high heat for a couple of minutes, add the one or two teaspoons of oil, and tilt the wok to swirl the oil around the bottom of the pan. Next, add the ingredients in the order suggested, and cook for the amount of time that the recipe calls for. As you put in the ingredients, continuously toss and stir them with a cooking spoon and spatula to enable everything to cook evenly, and to prevent any of the food from sticking to the pan or burning.

For stir-frying, all the ingredients *must* be cut up in small pieces. This makes it possible for the foods to be cooked thoroughly without being overdone.

On Your Tray

Because stir-frying is such a fast-moving process, it is important to have everything well organized. All the chopped ingredients should be close at hand in separate bowls or cups so you don't have to scramble around for them when the wok is hot. To make it easier for you to be organized, we provide a checklist in each stir-fry recipe called "On Your Tray." It will list what you need to have ready on a tray or your counter *before* you start to cook.

STEAMING

Another important Chinese cooking method is steaming. This is an especially good way to prepare vegetables because it retains their nutrients and natural flavors and keeps them moist.

A metal vegetable steamer will work for the recipes in this book. Our preference, however, is to use a wok and a bamboo steamer. You can buy a two- or three-piece Chinese bamboo steamer at most cookware shops. We use a three-piece steamer because this gives us two cooking levels plus the cover, but if you have a small family, a two-piece steamer will be fine. Make sure that the diameter of the steamer is the right size for the diameter of your wok; it should sit comfortably in the wok but still keep the food above the level of the water in the wok. A twelve-inch steamer will fit a fourteen-inch wok, or a ten-inch steamer will fit an eleven- or twelve-inch wok.

To steam in a wok, bring three or four inches of water to a boil in the wok and set the steamer, with the food already in it, into the wok. Set your timer according to the recipe, and steam away. Monitor the water level in the wok, and, if it gets too low, add more boiling water from a teakettle, which you should have heating on another burner.

To prevent food from sticking to the bamboo, or falling through the slats into the boiling water, either put a heatproof plate on the cooking rack to hold the food, or line the racks with lettuce leaves.

DEEP-FRYING

We use this particular Chinese cooking method very sparingly because it adds a lot of fat to any foods that are cooked this way. Chinese restaurants deep-fry batter-dipped foods and many appetizers, including egg rolls and dumplings. We generally avoid these foods or try to find lower-fat ways to prepare them.

Deep-frying involves cooking in a pan filled with several inches of very hot oil as you would use for French fries or tempura. You can use a wok, as we do, or a saucepan. Most Chinese recipes suggest using peanut oil, but we prefer canola oil because it is much lower in saturated fat.

When deep-frying, use a deep-frying thermometer and try to maintain a temperature of about 375° for the cooking oil by adjusting the heat as needed. If the temperature is too hot, the food will get too crusty; if it is too low, the food will absorb too much oil. Don't cook too many pieces at the same time or the temperature of the oil will be lowered, making the food greasier. Drain deep-fried food of excess oil before serving by placing it on paper towels.

CHINESE INGREDIENTS

You shouldn't have any trouble finding the ingredients called for in our recipes. Most are the same vegetables and grains you use all the time. Some special Chinese sauces and other ingredients are necessary, but we tell you about these, and where to find them, in the ingredient glossary at the end of this book.

Appetizers
and Dim Sum

RECITES

- *Tangerines and Snow Peas on Picks*
- *Eggplant Dip*
- *Spinach-Stuffed Mushrooms*
- *Grilled Dragon Kabobs*
- *Szechuan Pickled Cabbage*
- *Batter-Dipped Vegetables with Horseradish Dipping Sauce*
- *Steamed Squash Rolls*
- *Vegetarian Spring Rolls*
- *Curried Vegetable Puffs*
- *Crispy Vegetable-Filled Wontons*

• The Chinese like to pair contrasting colors, flavors, and textures. This easy-to-make cocktail hors d'oeuvre is a good example.

2 medium tangerines, peeled and separated into sections
12 snow peas, stems and strings removed

MARINADE

^{1}/$_4$ cup tangerine or orange juice
2 tablespoons orange marmalade
2 teaspoons low-sodium soy sauce
2 teaspoons sesame oil
1 teaspoon minced fresh garlic
1 teaspoon minced fresh ginger
^{1}/$_2$ teaspoon minced fresh green chili pepper

PREPARATION

1. Slice one edge of each tangerine section and slip out the seeds.
2. Slit the snow peas and separate them into 2 halves to make 24 pieces. Bring water to a boil in a small saucepan, add the snow peas, and blanch for 30 seconds. Drain and rinse in cold water to stop the cooking. Set aside.
3. Combine the marinade ingredients in a small bowl, stirring well to melt the marmalade. Pour over the tangerine sections and marinate for 1 hour.

ASSEMBLY

1. Drain the tangerine sections.
2. Wrap one snow pea half around each section of tangerine and secure with a toothpick.
3. Chill until ready to serve.

Tangerines and Snow Peas on Picks

•

Makes 24 pieces

Eggplant Dip

•

Makes 2 cups

• This colorful, mildly spicy eggplant dip carries the distinctive flavor of its coriander garnish. If you are not a coriander fan, substitute parsley.

1 small eggplant, peeled and cut into $^1/_2$-inch cubes
1 teaspoon salt

SEASONINGS

1 teaspoon minced fresh ginger
1 teaspoon minced fresh garlic
1 teaspoon minced fresh green chili pepper
$^1/_2$ cup finely chopped onion

VEGETABLES

1 stalk celery, cut into $^1/_4$-inch cubes
$^1/_2$ red bell pepper, seeds and ribs removed, and cut into $^1/_4$-inch cubes

SAUCE

2 tablespoons rice vinegar
1 tablespoon low-sodium soy sauce
1 tablespoon sesame oil

ADDITIONAL INGREDIENTS

1 tablespoon canola oil
2 tablespoons chopped fresh coriander leaves for garnish

PREPARATION

1. Toss the eggplant with the salt and set aside for 30 minutes. Rinse in cold water and drain.
2. Combine the seasonings with the celery in a bowl.
3. Combine the red bell pepper with the rinsed eggplant in a bowl.
4. Combine the sauce ingredients in a small bowl.
5. Assemble your cooking tray.

ON YOUR TRAY

Canola oil
Bowl of seasonings and celery

Bowl of eggplant and red bell pepper
Bowl of sauce

COOKING

1. Heat a nonstick wok over high heat for 2 minutes.
2. Add the canola oil and the seasonings and celery. Stir-fry for 2 minutes.
3. Add the eggplant and red bell pepper and stir-fry for 3 minutes.
4. Add the sauce and stir to combine.
5. Transfer to a small serving bowl and sprinkle with the coriander.
6. Serve chilled or at room temperature, with crackers.

Spinach-
Stuffed
Mushrooms

●

Makes 24
stuffed
mushroom
caps

● These black bean–flavored, slightly spicy stuffed mushrooms make an appealing appetizer course for a small dinner party.

24 fresh mushrooms, each about 2 inches in diameter

FILLING

1 teaspoon minced fresh garlic
1 teaspoon minced fresh ginger
1 teaspoon minced fresh green chili pepper
$^{1}/_{2}$ cup finely chopped onion
8 ounces fresh spinach, washed and tough stems removed
1 egg, lightly beaten
1 tablespoon black bean sauce

ADDITIONAL INGREDIENTS

2 teaspoons canola oil
2 cups Vegetable Broth (page 49)
2 teaspoons cornstarch dissolved in 1 tablespoon cold water
2 tablespoons chopped fresh parsley for garnish

PREPARATION

1. Remove the stems from the mushroom caps and finely chop the stems. Set the mushroom caps aside to be stuffed with the filling.
2. Combine the garlic, ginger, and chili pepper in a small bowl.
3. Assemble your cooking tray for preparing the filling.

ON YOUR TRAY

Canola oil

Bowl of garlic, ginger, and chili
   pepper

Bowl of chopped onion

Bowl of chopped mushroom stems

Bowl of spinach

Beaten egg

Black bean sauce

COOKING THE FILLING

1. Heat a nonstick wok over high heat for 2 minutes.
2. Add 1 teaspoon of the canola oil, then the garlic, ginger, and chili pepper and stir-fry for 15 seconds.
3. Add the onion and stir-fry for 15 seconds.
4. Add the chopped mushroom stems and stir-fry for 1 minute.
5. Add the spinach and stir until wilted, about 1 minute.
6. Transfer the spinach mixture to a bowl and set aside to cool for a few minutes. Stir in the beaten egg and black bean sauce.

COOKING THE MUSHROOM CAPS

1. Mound a spoonful of the spinach filling into each mushroom cap.
2. Heat the remaining teaspoon of the canola oil in a large nonstick skillet.
3. Arrange the stuffed mushroom caps in one layer in the skillet and brown the bottoms for about 30 seconds.
4. Pour in the vegetable broth, cover, turn the heat to medium-low, and cook for 8 minutes.
5. Remove the cover, stir in the cornstarch mixture, and cook until the sauce has thickened and is glossy.
6. Transfer the mushrooms and sauce to a serving platter and sprinkle with the parsley.

• 8 fresh mushroom caps, each about 2 inches in diameter
8 cherry tomatoes
1 green bell pepper, ribs and seeds removed, and cut into 8 (1 1/2-inch)
    squares
8 broccoli florets
1 medium onion, peeled and cut into 8 wedges

MARINADE

1/2 cup chopped scallions
1/2 cup chopped onion
1/2 cup low-sodium soy sauce
1/2 cup rice vinegar
2 tablespoons sesame oil
1/4 cup brown sugar
2 tablespoons chili paste

1. Thread the vegetables on eight 8-inch bamboo skewers.
2. Combine the marinade ingredients in a food processor and process to make
   a thin paste.
3. Place the kabobs in a 9 × 13-inch pan. Pour the marinade over the kabobs.
4. Cover and refrigerate at least 4 hours, turning the skewers occasionally.
5. Place the kabobs on a medium-hot grill and cook about 5 minutes on
   each side.

• This tangy salad is similar to the pickled vegetables brought out by many Chinese restaurants as a predinner relish. It can be served as an appetizer or as a salad. You can store pickled cabbage in the refrigerator, covered, for up to two weeks.

1/2 head green cabbage, cored and cut into 1-inch pieces
2 carrots, peeled and cut into 1/2-inch slices
1 red bell pepper, seeds and ribs removed, and cut into 1-inch pieces

MARINADE

3 cloves garlic, peeled and crushed
6 slices fresh ginger, each about the size of a quarter, peeled
4 to 6 dried red chili peppers, broken in half
1 quart cold water
1 cup sugar
1 cup rice vinegar

1. Combine the cabbage, carrots, and red pepper in a large glass or stainless steel bowl.
2. Combine the ingredients for the marinade and stir to dissolve the sugar.
3. Pour the marinade over the vegetables and stir to mix well.
4. Place a plate over the vegetables and a weight on top of the plate.
5. Refrigerate for three days to allow the flavors to develop, turning the vegetables occasionally.
6. Remove the dried red chili peppers, ginger, and garlic, and drain before serving.

Szechuan Pickled Cabbage

•

Makes about 6 cups

Batter-
Dipped
Vegetables
with
Horse-
radish
Dipping
Sauce

•

Makes
4 to 6
appetizer
servings

• This is one of our few deep-fry recipes. It is so good that we had to include it, even though it's not lowfat. These batter-dipped vegetables can be served as an hors d'oeuvre or an appetizer course or, if you increase the recipe and add other vegetables (one-inch squares of red and green bell peppers, one-inch segments of scallion, snow peas, etc.), you have a Chinese version of tempura.

BATTER

1 1/2 cups warm water (90° to 100°)
1/2 teaspoon sugar
1 package active dry yeast
1 1/2 cups all-purpose flour
1 tablespoon canola oil
1/2 teaspoon salt

VEGETABLES

8 broccoli florets
8 cauliflower florets
8 mushroom caps, each 2 inches in diameter
2 small onions, each peeled and cut into 4 wedges

ADDITIONAL INGREDIENTS

2 to 3 cups canola oil
Horseradish Dipping Sauce (recipe follows)

PREPARATION

1. In a small bowl, combine 1/4 cup of the warm water with the sugar. Sprinkle the yeast over the water and set aside for a few minutes while the yeast dissolves.

2. Combine 1 cup of the flour, the remaining 1 1/4 cups of warm water, the dissolved yeast mixture, oil, and salt in a large mixing bowl.
3. Cover and set aside to rest for at least 1 hour. (The batter can be refrigerated overnight. But be sure to bring it back to room temperature before proceeding with the recipe.)
4. Add the remaining 1/2 cup of the flour to the batter and mix well.

COOKING

1. Heat the oil in a wok to 375°. (Use a deep-frying thermometer to make sure the correct temperature is maintained.)
2. Preheat the oven to 225°.
3. Dip the vegetables into the batter and fry a few at a time until golden. Drain on paper towels. Place on a rack on a baking sheet in the warm oven while frying the remaining vegetables.
4. Serve warm with the horseradish dipping sauce.

HORSERADISH DIPPING SAUCE

1/4 cup low-sodium soy sauce
1/4 cup Vegetable Broth (page 49) or water
1 tablespoon prepared horseradish
1 teaspoon sugar
1/2 teaspoon Chinese hot oil
1 tablespoon chopped scallion

1. Combine all the ingredients and pour into a small dish.
2. Serve with the batter-fried vegetables.

Steamed Squash Rolls

• These steamed rolls are especially good as an accompaniment for a soup entrée. If the quantity is more than you'll need, just halve the recipe.

1 pound prepared white bread dough (available in the supermarket freezer section)

Makes 16 to 18 rolls

FILLING

2 cups butternut squash, peeled, seeded, and cut into 1-inch cubes
1 teaspoon minced fresh garlic
1 teaspoon minced fresh ginger
1 teaspoon low-sodium soy sauce
1 teaspoon minced fresh green chili pepper
1 teaspoon orange zest

ADDITIONAL INGREDIENTS

1 tablespoon sesame seeds, lightly toasted in a dry skillet over medium heat
18 (3-inch) squares waxed paper or parchment paper

PREPARATION

1. Boil the squash until tender, drain, and purée in a food processor or blender. If the squash seems watery after puréeing, cook for a few minutes in a saucepan to evaporate some of the liquid. Place in a mixing bowl.
2. Combine the other filling ingredients in a bowl, add to the puréed squash, and mix well.
3. Thaw the bread dough. Place it in a bowl in a warm place to rise according to package directions.

1. Break off 1 1/2- to 2-inch pieces of the bread dough and roll into balls.
2. Place each ball of dough on a lightly floured surface and flatten to a 3 1/2- to 4-inch circle.
3. Place a rounded tablespoon of the filling in the center of each dough circle, pull up the sides, and pinch to close.
4. Place the rolls pinched-side down on the squares of paper and set aside in a warm place for 30 minutes to rise. Arrange the rolls on the racks of a bamboo steamer. (Leave enough room between the rolls so they don't stick together when steaming.) Cover the steamer.

COOKING

1. Bring 3 to 4 inches of water to a boil in a wok, and place the covered steamer on top.
2. Steam for 15 minutes. Serve immediately.

• This recipe was devised with the idea that some portion of the spring rolls could be frozen and used another time. Once you are geared up to cook spring rolls, you might as well do a fair number of them. Otherwise, just halve the recipe.

If you want to try a lower-fat alternative to these deep-fried spring rolls, use the instructions that follow for the sautéed and baked ones instead. They will not be as crispy, but they will be decidedly lower in fat.

Makes
18 rolls

SEASONINGS

1 tablespoon minced fresh garlic
1 tablespoon minced fresh ginger
1 tablespoon minced fresh green chili pepper
1 cup chopped onion

VEGETABLES

4 cups shredded green cabbage
1 cup thinly sliced celery
1 green bell pepper, seeds and ribs removed, and cut into thin slivers
2 cups sliced fresh mushrooms
1 cup coarsely grated carrots
2 cups fresh bean sprouts, washed and drained

ADDITIONAL INGREDIENTS

2 tablespoons canola oil
1 teaspoon salt
2 tablespoons hoisin sauce
18 spring roll wrappers
2 eggs, lightly beaten with 2 tablespoons cold water
2 cups canola oil for deep-frying
Duck sauce for dipping

PREPARING THE FILLING

1. Combine the seasonings in a bowl.
2. Place each vegetable in a separate bowl.
3. Assemble your cooking tray.

ON YOUR TRAY

2 tablespoons canola oil
Bowl of seasonings
Bowl of cabbage
Bowl of celery
Bowl of green pepper

Bowl of mushrooms
Bowl of carrots
Bowl of bean sprouts
Salt
Hoisin sauce

COOKING THE FILLING

1. Heat a nonstick wok over high heat for 2 minutes.
2. Add 1 tablespoon of the canola oil, then the seasonings, and stir-fry for 30 seconds.
3. Add the cabbage and stir-fry for 2 minutes.
4. Add the celery and stir-fry for 2 minutes.
5. Add the remaining tablespoon of the canola oil if the food is sticking to the wok, and add the green pepper and stir-fry for 1 minute.
6. Add the mushrooms and stir-fry for 1 minute.
7. Add the carrots and stir-fry for 1 minute.
8. Add the bean sprouts, then the salt, and stir to mix well.
9. Remove the vegetables to a colander and drain.
10. Place the drained vegetable mixture in a large bowl and add the hoisin sauce. Stir to mix well.
11. Set aside for 20 to 30 minutes, or until the mixture is cool enough to handle.

(continues)

1. Carefully separate the spring roll wrappers. Lightly cover the wrappers with a towel so they don't dry out.
2. Working one at a time, place a wrapper on a work surface and spoon $1/3$ cup of the vegetable mixture in the center of the wrapper. Using a pastry brush, coat the outer edges of the wrapper with some of the beaten egg.
3. Fold the wrapper from the bottom to cover the filling. Fold the two sides in toward the center and continue rolling until you have a cylinder. The egg will seal the edges. Place the completed spring roll, seam-side down, on a platter. Lightly cover with a towel while preparing the rest of the spring rolls.

COOKING THE SPRING ROLLS

1. Heat the 2 cups canola oil in a wok until the temperature reaches 375°. (Use a deep-frying thermometer to make sure the correct temperature is maintained.)
2. Fry 2 spring rolls at a time, gently turning them after 2 minutes. Cook an additional 2 minutes, or until the rolls are golden brown. Remove with a slotted spoon and drain on paper towels for 1 minute before placing them on a baking rack. (This will prevent them from becoming soggy.) The spring rolls can be kept warm in a 225° oven, or wrapped well and refrigerated or frozen if you do not want to serve them immediately. Reheat frozen rolls at 375° for 20 minutes.
3. Serve with the duck sauce.

ALTERNATIVE COOKING INSTRUCTIONS FOR SAUTÉED/BAKED SPRING ROLLS

1. Preheat the oven to 375°. Heat a nonstick skillet over medium-high heat.
2. Add 1 tablespoon canola oil and swirl it around the bottom of the pan.

3. Sauté the spring rolls, 2 at a time, turning them over to brown them on all sides. Add more oil if the spring rolls begin to stick to the skillet.

4. Place the browned spring rolls on a rack on a baking sheet to let the excess oil drip off. Bake for 12 minutes to heat them through. These spring rolls also can be frozen for later use.

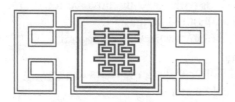

Curried Vegetable Puffs

• These delightful, tiny pastry turnovers are ideal to serve with cocktails.

2 cups Curried Vegetable Pie filling (see note)
Foolproof Pastry Dough for 2 (9-inch) pie shells (recipe follows)
1 egg white, lightly beaten with 1 tablespoon cold water

Makes 36 puffs

PREPARATION

1. Roll out the pastry dough on a lightly floured surface to $^{1}/_{8}$ inch thick.
2. Cut out 3-inch rounds with a biscuit cutter. (Gather scraps and reroll after each cutting to use all of the dough.)
3. Place a rounded teaspoon of the curried vegetable pie filling in the center of each pastry round.
4. Fold the pastry in half, crimping the edges together. (It helps to dampen the edge with a little cold water.)
5. Brush the top of each turnover with the egg white and prick the top with the tines of a fork. Place on an ungreased baking sheet.

COOKING

1. Preheat the oven to 375°.
2. Bake for 15 minutes, or until the pastries are golden brown.
3. The puffs can be frozen fully baked and reheated at 350° for 12 to 15 minutes.

NOTE   This is one-half the quantity used in the Curried Vegetable Pie recipe (pages 142–143).

FOOLPROOF PASTRY DOUGH
Makes 2 (9-inch) pastry shells

The inclusion of lemon juice makes this crust easy to work with.

2 cups all-purpose flour
2 teaspoons sugar
1 teaspoon salt
14 tablespoons chilled margarine or butter
2 teaspoons lemon juice
3 to 4 tablespoons cold water

1. Combine the flour, sugar, and salt in a large mixing bowl.
2. Work the margarine into the flour using your fingers, a pastry blender, or a food processor. (If using a processor, do not overprocess or the dough will be tough.) The mixture should look like coarse cornmeal.
3. Add the lemon juice and enough cold water to form a ball with the dough.
4. Wrap in plastic wrap and refrigerate for at least 30 minutes before rolling out.

• Fried wontons, served with a choice of duck sauce or hot mustard for dipping, make a delicious hors d'oeuvre. To make life simpler for the cook, they can be made ahead and frozen, uncooked, to be deep-fried when ready to serve.

•

*Makes 36
wontons*

SEASONINGS

1 teaspoon minced fresh ginger
1 teaspoon minced fresh garlic
$^1/_2$ cup finely chopped onion

VEGETABLES

10 ounces fresh spinach, washed and tough stems removed
8 dried Chinese mushrooms, soaked in hot water for 30 minutes
$^1/_4$ cup finely chopped water chestnuts
2 cups grated fresh parsnips

ADDITIONAL INGREDIENTS

1 tablespoon canola oil
1 tablespoon low-sodium soy sauce
36 wonton wrappers
2 cups of canola oil for deep-frying
Duck sauce or Chinese mustard for dipping

PREPARING THE FILLING

1. Combine the seasonings in a small bowl.
2. Coarsely chop the spinach and place it in a bowl.
3. Drain the mushrooms. Remove the stems and discard them. Finely chop the caps and place in a bowl with the water chestnuts.
4. Assemble your cooking tray.

Canola oil
Bowl of seasonings
Bowl of parsnips
Bowl of spinach

Bowl of mushrooms and water
  chestnuts
Soy sauce

COOKING THE FILLING

1. Heat a nonstick wok over high heat for 2 minutes.
2. Add the canola oil and the seasonings. Stir-fry for 30 seconds.
3. Add the parsnips and stir-fry for 1 minute.
4. Add the spinach and stir until wilted, about 30 seconds.
5. Stir in the mushrooms and water chestnuts and combine well.
6. Stir in the soy sauce and remove the wok from the burner.
7. Place the vegetable mixture in a colander and allow to drain and cool before filling the wonton wrappers.

ASSEMBLY

1. Place a wonton wrapper on a work surface and place a rounded teaspoon of the filling in the center. (Keep the remaining wrappers covered with a towel while you're working so they don't dry out.)
2. Using your fingers, dampen the outer edge of the wonton with cold water and fold the wrapper in half covering the filling and forming a triangle. Pinch the edges together to seal.
3. For each filled wrapper, bring the two wings of the triangle together, overlap them, moisten with a little cold water, and pinch to seal.

(continues)

1. Preheat the oven to 225°.
2. Heat the 2 cups canola oil in a wok to a temperature of 375°. (Use a deep-frying thermometer to make sure the correct temperature is maintained.)
3. Fry the wontons about 6 at a time until golden brown, about 3 minutes for each batch. (Do not crowd them or they won't brown nicely.) Drain on paper towels. Keep the cooked wontons warm on a baking rack over a baking sheet in a low oven while frying the remaining batches.
4. Place wontons on a serving tray with a small dish of either duck sauce or Chinese mustard.

NOTE   To freeze, place uncooked wontons, uncovered, on a cookie sheet in the freezer for about 1 hour. (Do not let them touch or they will stick together.) When frozen, transfer them to a plastic bag and store in the freezer until ready to use—fried, as an hors d'oeuvre, or boiled, in Vegetable Wonton Soup (page 48). It is not necessary to thaw them before using in a recipe. They can be kept in the freezer for up to 3 months.

Soups

RECIPES

- Snow Pea and Mushroom Egg Drop Soup

- Hot and Sour Vegetable Soup

- Cauliflower Soup with Carrots and Peas

- Sweet Potato–Green Chili Soup

- Golden Squash Soup with Leeks

- Spicy Vegetable Chowder

- Sunshine Pepper Soup

- Velvet Corn and Lima Bean Soup

- Asparagus-Garlic Soup

- Chilled Pineapple-Melon Soup

- Vegetable Wonton Soup

- Vegetable Broth

• Egg drop soup is a Chinese favorite. This variation adds snow peas, mushrooms, and a spark of hot pepper sauce. We have reduced the cholesterol count by using just one whole egg plus one egg white.

1 tablespoon low-sodium soy sauce
1 tablespoon dry sherry
$^{1}/_{2}$ teaspoon hot red pepper sauce, such as Tabasco
$^{1}/_{4}$ teaspoon white pepper
4 cups Vegetable Broth (page 49)
2 cups fresh mushrooms, cleaned, trimmed, and sliced
1 cup fresh snow peas, stems and strings removed, and cut into slivers
1 whole egg plus 1 egg white, lightly beaten
1 scallion, both white and green parts, trimmed and chopped for garnish

1. Combine the soy sauce, sherry, red pepper sauce, and white pepper in a small bowl.
2. Bring the broth to a boil in a large saucepan.
3. Add the mushrooms, cover, and simmer for 5 minutes.
4. Remove the cover, add the snow peas, and bring to a boil. Cook for 1 minute.
5. Stir in the soy sauce mixture. Reduce the heat to low, and gently blend in the egg, forming ribbons of egg in the soup.
6. Serve in individual bowls and garnish each with a sprinkling of chopped scallion.

Snow Pea and Mushroom Egg Drop Soup

•

Makes 4 servings

Hot and

Sour

Vegetable

Soup

•

Makes 4 to
6 servings

• Chili paste and Chinese hot oil are the "hot" and rice vinegar is the "sour." The leeks add their delicate flavor and the bean curd its special texture.

2 leeks
1 tablespoon minced fresh ginger
1 tablespoon minced fresh garlic
8 dried Chinese mushrooms, soaked in hot water for 30 minutes
2 carrots, cut into $^1/_2$-inch cubes
1 stalk celery, cut into $^1/_2$-inch cubes
3 tablespoons low-sodium soy sauce
3 tablespoons rice vinegar
1 teaspoon honey
2 teaspoons chili paste
1 teaspoon Chinese hot oil
1 tablespoon sesame oil
6 cups Vegetable Broth (page 49)
1 cup shredded cabbage
1 egg, lightly beaten
2 cups fresh spinach, washed and tough stems removed
8 ounces soft bean curd, cut into $^1/_2$-inch cubes

PREPARATION

1. Trim the root ends of the leeks. Cut off and discard the upper green parts, about 2 inches above the white bulbs. Make a cross slit about 1 inch deep in the direction of the bulb end of each leek. Rinse the leeks well under cold water to remove any sand that has lodged in the layers. Thinly slice the bulb. Combine this with the ginger and garlic in a bowl.

2. Drain the mushrooms. Remove the stems and discard them. Cut the caps into thin shreds.
3. Combine the carrots and celery with the mushrooms in a bowl.
4. Combine the soy sauce, rice vinegar, honey, chili paste, and Chinese hot oil in a small bowl.

COOKING

1. Heat the sesame oil in a large saucepan.
2. Add the leeks, ginger, and garlic and stir to coat with the oil. Cover and reduce the heat to low. Cook for 5 minutes, stirring occasionally.
3. Remove the cover, turn the heat to high, and add the broth.
4. Bring the broth to a boil and add the carrots, celery, and mushrooms. Cover and simmer for 6 minutes.
5. Add the cabbage and simmer, covered, for 4 minutes.
6. Stir in the soy sauce mixture, then the beaten egg, forming thin shreds of egg as you stir.
7. Add the spinach and stir to wilt.
8. Gently add the bean curd and stir to combine.
9. Serve in individual soup bowls.

*Cauliflower
Soup with
Carrots and
Peas*

•

Makes 4
servings

• The secret to creating this low-calorie yet creamy soup is the puréed cauliflower—there's no need to add cream. Coriander provides this soup's unique flavor.

3 cups Vegetable Broth (page 49)
1 cup chopped onion
1 teaspoon minced fresh ginger
1 head cauliflower, coarsely chopped (Reserve 1 cup small florets before chopping)
1 large carrot, peeled and cut into $^1/_2$-inch cubes
1 stalk celery, trimmed and cut into $^1/_2$-inch cubes
1 cup frozen green peas, thawed
1 tablespoon dry sherry
2 tablespoons chopped fresh coriander leaves

1. Bring the broth to a boil in a saucepan.
2. Add the onion, ginger, and chopped cauliflower to the pan. Cover and cook until the cauliflower is tender, about 12 minutes.
3. Purée the soup in a food processor or blender. Return the puréed soup to the stove and bring to a boil.
4. Add the carrot and celery, and bring to a boil. Cover and simmer for 3 minutes. Remove the cover and add the reserved cauliflower florets and the peas. Cover and cook for 3 minutes more.
5. Remove the cover, add the sherry and coriander, stir, and serve.

*Sweet
Potato–
Green
Chili Soup*

•

*Makes 4
servings*

- $^1/_2$ pound sweet potatoes, peeled and cut into $^1/_2$-inch cubes
1 cup chopped onion
1 tablespoon minced fresh garlic
1 tablespoon minced fresh ginger
1 tablespoon minced green chili pepper
2 teaspoons canola oil
1 cup canned crushed tomatoes
3 cups Vegetable Broth (page 49)
Salt to taste

PREPARATION

1. Bring water to a boil in a saucepan and cook the potatoes until tender, about 3 minutes. Drain and set aside.
2. Combine the onion, garlic, ginger, and chili pepper in a bowl.

COOKING

1. Heat the canola oil in a 2-quart saucepan.
2. Add the onion mixture and sauté for 1 minute, stirring continuously.
3. Add the tomatoes and broth, and bring to a boil. Cover and reduce the heat to simmer. Cook for 10 minutes.
4. Stir in the cooked sweet potatoes.
5. Add salt to taste.
6. Cook an additional 1 minute to heat through.

Golden
Squash
Soup with
Leeks

•

Makes 4
servings

• 3 leeks
1 tablespoon low-sodium soy sauce
1 tablespoon dry sherry
$^1/_2$ teaspoon Chinese hot oil
1 teaspoon canola oil
1 teaspoon minced fresh garlic
1 cup chopped onion
4 cups Vegetable Broth (page 49)
1 large potato, peeled and cut into $^1/_2$-inch cubes
2 small yellow summer squash, cut into $^1/_2$-inch cubes
1 stalk celery, chopped
$^1/_4$ cup chopped fresh parsley

PREPARATION

1. Trim the root ends of the leeks. Cut off and discard the upper green parts, about 2 inches above the white bulbs. Make a cross slit about 1 inch deep in the direction of the bulb end of each leek. Rinse the leeks well under cold running water to remove any sand that has lodged in the layers. Thinly slice the leeks.
2. Combine the soy sauce, sherry, and Chinese hot oil in a small bowl.

COOKING

1. Heat the canola oil in a saucepan for 30 seconds.
2. Add the garlic, onion, and leeks, stir to coat in the oil, and cover. Reduce the heat to simmer, and cook for 5 minutes, stirring occasionally.
3. Add the broth, then the potatoes, and raise the heat to medium-high. Cover, bring to a boil, and cook for 5 minutes, or until the potatoes are tender.

4. Place the soup in a food processor and purée.
5. Return the soup to the stove and bring to a boil again.
6. Add the squash and the celery, cover, and cook for 5 minutes.
7. Remove from the heat and stir in the soy sauce mixture, then the parsley. Serve in individual bowls.

●

3 tablespoons low-sodium soy sauce
2 tablespoons dry sherry
$^1/_2$ teaspoon hot red pepper sauce, such as Tabasco
$^1/_2$ teaspoon crushed red pepper
Salt to taste

SOUP BASE

3 cups Vegetable Broth (page 49)
1 tablespoon minced fresh garlic
1 medium onion, chopped
1 cup broccoli florets
1 cup cauliflower florets
1 cup chopped carrots

ADDITIONAL INGREDIENTS

2 carrots, cut into $^1/_8$-inch slices
2 celery stalks, cut into $^1/_8$-inch slices
1 small zucchini, cut into $^1/_8$-inch slices
3 tablespoons minced fresh coriander leaves

1. Combine the soy sauce, sherry, red pepper sauce, crushed red pepper, and salt to taste in a small bowl. Set aside.
2. In a large saucepan, bring the soup base ingredients to a boil, cover, and cook for 20 minutes.
3. Transfer the soup base to a blender or food processor and purée. Return puréed soup base to the saucepan.
4. In a small saucepan, bring water to a boil, add the sliced carrots, and boil for 2 minutes.

5. Add the celery and boil for 1 minute.
6. Add the zucchini and boil an additional minute.
7. Drain the vegetables and add them to the soup base in the large saucepan.
8. Bring the soup to a boil and add the soy sauce mixture. Taste to see if additional salt is needed.
9. Stir until the soup is heated through, about 3 minutes.
10. Stir in the coriander and serve.

Sunshine Pepper Soup

•

• The yellow peppers are the "sunshine" in this soup.

4 yellow bell peppers
$1/2$ cup chopped onion
1 teaspoon minced fresh garlic
1 teaspoon minced fresh ginger
2 teaspoons canola oil
3 cups Vegetable Broth (page 49)
$1/4$ teaspoon white pepper
Salt to taste
2 tablespoons minced fresh coriander leaves for garnish

PREPARATION

1. Broil the peppers on a baking sheet, placed 3 inches from the source of heat. Turn the peppers as the skin blisters and blackens. It will take about 12 to 15 minutes to blacken the entire pepper.
2. Transfer the peppers to a brown paper bag and close tightly.
3. Open the bag after 10 to 15 minutes, and remove the peppers. Slip off the skins. (Don't worry if all the charred skin doesn't come off. This will add flavor to the soup.)
4. Cut the peppers in half, and remove the seeds and ribs.
5. Place the peppers in a food processor bowl and purée.
6. Combine the onion, garlic, and ginger in a small bowl.

COOKING

1. Heat a nonstick wok over high heat for 2 minutes.
2. Add the canola oil and the onion mixture and stir-fry for 1 minute.
3. Add the puréed peppers, the broth, and white pepper, cover, and simmer for 10 minutes. Salt to taste, spoon into individual bowls, and sprinkle with the coriander.

• This is a variation on the classic velvet corn soup, with the addition of lima beans.

1 teaspoon canola oil
1 teaspoon minced fresh ginger
1/2 cup chopped onion
4 cups Vegetable Broth (page 49)
1 (16-ounce) can creamed corn
2 egg whites, lightly beaten
1 cup drained canned baby corn ears, cut into 1-inch pieces
1 cup frozen lima beans, cooked
1 tablespoon chopped fresh parsley for garnish

1. Heat the canola oil in a saucepan for 30 seconds.
2. Add the ginger and onion and sauté for 30 seconds.
3. Pour in the broth, cover, turn heat to medium, and cook for 5 minutes.
4. Remove the cover and stir in the creamed corn.
5. Slowly pour in the egg whites, stirring the soup with a fork or chopstick to form thin shreds of egg.
6. Stir in the baby corn pieces and lima beans and cook until heated through, about 3 minutes.
7. Serve in individual bowls and sprinkle with the parsley.

Velvet Corn and Lima Bean Soup

Makes 4 servings

• Asparagus soup can be bland, but with garlic, onion, and hot pepper sauce, this one has an attitude—a Chinese attitude.

3 cups Vegetable Broth (page 49)
1 cup dry white wine
2 pounds fresh asparagus, cleaned, trimmed, and cut into 2-inch lengths
2 tablespoons minced fresh garlic
1 cup chopped onion
2 tablespoons low-sodium soy sauce
1 tablespoon dry sherry
1/2 teaspoon hot red pepper sauce, such as Tabasco
1 red bell pepper, seeds and ribs removed, and finely chopped
1 tablespoon lemon zest for garnish

1. Bring the broth and wine to a boil in a saucepan.
2. Add the asparagus, garlic, and onion, and bring to a boil. Cover, reduce the heat to low, and simmer for 20 minutes.
3. Transfer the soup to a food processor or blender and purée.
4. Return the puréed soup to the saucepan and bring to a boil.
5. Season with the soy sauce, sherry, and red pepper sauce.
6. Stir in the red bell pepper and boil for 1 minute.
7. Serve in individual bowls and sprinkle each serving with the lemon zest.

- 1 large ripe cantaloupe or honeydew melon, peeled, seeds removed, and cut into chunks
  1 1/2 cups orange juice
  1/4 cup dry sherry
  1 teaspoon minced fresh ginger
  1 teaspoon cinnamon
  1/2 pineapple, peeled, cored, and cut into 1/4-inch cubes (about 2 cups)
  Sprigs of fresh mint for garnish

1. Place the melon in a food processor or blender and purée.
2. Pour the purée into a bowl and stir in the orange juice, sherry, ginger, and cinnamon.
3. Add the pineapple and refrigerate at least 3 hours to allow the flavors to develop.
4. Garnish with the mint sprigs before serving.

Chilled Pineapple-Melon Soup

Makes 4 servings

• Wonton soup is another Chinese favorite, and this vegetarian version can be served as a main dish, with squash rolls or a good bread, and a salad.

8 dried Chinese mushrooms, soaked in hot water for 30 minutes
24 uncooked vegetable-filled wontons (pages 30–31)
2 quarts Vegetable Broth (facing page)
2 cups coarsely chopped bok choy
$1/2$ cup sliced water chestnuts
$1/2$ red bell pepper, seeds and ribs removed, and cut into $1/2$-inch squares
2 scallions, both white and green parts, thinly sliced
3 tablespoons low-sodium soy sauce
3 tablespoons dry sherry
White pepper to taste

PREPARATION

1. Drain the mushrooms, and remove and discard the stems. Slice the caps into $1/8$-inch strips.
2. Bring several quarts of water to a boil in a large stockpot and carefully drop in the wontons.
3. Bring the water to a boil again, turn the heat to medium, and gently boil the wontons for 5 to 6 minutes. Drain and set aside until ready to add to the soup.

COOKING

1. Bring the broth to a boil.
2. Add the remaining ingredients, except for the wontons. Cover, turn the heat to medium, and cook for 6 to 8 minutes.
3. Remove the cover, add the cooked wontons, and simmer gently just to heat the wontons through, 2 to 3 minutes.

• You can, of course, buy vegetable broths at your market, but most of them are made with a lot of salt—just look at the nutrition information on the label. This is a lower-sodium version that is easy to make at home.

1 cup dry white wine
4 large onions, peeled and quartered
6 large carrots, peeled and sliced
4 celery stalks, sliced (include the leaves)
1 large parsnip, peeled and sliced
1 cup tightly packed fresh parsley, with stems
1 tablespoon fresh thyme, or 1 teaspoon dried
3 bay leaves
5 cloves garlic, peeled and slightly crushed
8 to 10 black peppercorns
2 teaspoons low-sodium soy sauce

1. Combine all the ingredients in a large heavy stockpot, and bring to a boil.
2. Partially cover, reduce the heat to low, and simmer for 1 hour.
3. Strain out the vegetables. Taste. If the flavor seems weak, boil uncovered to reduce the broth. This will make it more flavorful.
4. You can store the broth in the refrigerator for up to 5 days or in the freezer for up to 3 months.

NOTE   In some of the recipes that call for $1/2$ cup or less vegetable broth, we give you the option of substituting water for the broth. It is preferable to use the vegetable broth because it adds to the flavor of a recipe, but it may not be worth the effort to buy or make it for such a small quantity if you don't have it on hand.

Salads

RECITES

- Dragon Tomato Salad
- Asparagus Salad with Cellophane Noodles
- Broccoli Salad with Grapefruit Dressing
- Curried Corn and Red Pepper Salad
- Spinach and Kiwi Salad
- Warm Cucumber Salad with Lemon-Sesame Dressing
- Cucumber and Mandarin Orange Salad
- Mango Salad with Creamy Cucumber Dressing
- Minted Fruit Salad
- Carrot-Pineapple Relish

• The Chinese like to mix contrasting tastes and textures in their foods, a little yin with a bit of yang. You can see that in the ingredients of this easy salad.

3 large ripe tomatoes, peeled, seeded, and coarsely chopped
1 stalk celery, cut into $1/4$-inch cubes
$1/4$ cup finely chopped onion
$1/4$ cup sliced water chestnuts
1 teaspoon minced ginger
1 tablespoon minced fresh green chili pepper
$1/4$ cup rice vinegar
2 tablespoons sugar
2 tablespoons chopped fresh chives for garnish

1. Combine the tomatoes, celery, onion, water chestnuts, ginger, and chili pepper in a bowl.
2. Combine the rice vinegar and sugar in a small saucepan and bring to a boil. Stir to dissolve the sugar.
3. Pour the hot rice vinegar dressing over the tomato mixture. Stir well to combine, and refrigerate for 2 to 3 hours or overnight to allow the flavors to develop.
4. When ready to serve, sprinkle the salad with the chives.

Dragon Tomato Salad

•

Makes 4 servings

• Cellophane noodles, sometimes called bean threads or Chinese vermicelli, are delicate, translucent noodles made from mung beans. If you can't find them, use thin Italian pasta (vermicelli or angel hair) and cook it according to the package directions, rather than soaking it in hot water as called for in this recipe.

1 1/2 pounds thin fresh asparagus spears, trimmed and
    cut into 2-inch lengths
1 (2-ounce) package cellophane noodles
1/2 red bell pepper, ribs and seeds removed, and cut
    into 1/2-inch squares
4 scallions, both white and green parts, trimmed and chopped
1/2 cup sliced water chestnuts
1/2 cup sliced red radishes
1 tablespoon sesame oil
3 tablespoons rice vinegar
1 tablespoon chili paste
Salt to taste
2 tablespoons chopped fresh coriander leaves for garnish

1. Bring water to a boil in a large saucepan and cook the asparagus for 2 minutes. Drain and rinse in cold water. Set aside.
2. Place the cellophane noodles in a large bowl. Pour boiling water over the noodles and allow to soak for at least 10 minutes to soften. Drain and set aside.
3. Combine the asparagus, noodles, red bell pepper, scallions, water chestnuts, and radishes in a large bowl.
4. Combine the sesame oil, rice vinegar, and chili paste, and toss with the vegetables and noodles. Add salt to taste.
5. Arrange the salad in a serving bowl and top with the coriander.

● This surprising combination of broccoli and grapefruit juice dressing is given extra zest by the Chinese hot oil. If you are looking for a change of pace from everyday salads, this will get your attention.

3 cups small broccoli florets
1 cup sliced mushrooms
1 cup fresh grapefruit juice
2 tablespoons rice vinegar
1 teaspoon sugar
1/2 teaspoon Chinese hot oil
4 lettuce leaves, washed and dried
2 tablespoons pine nuts, lightly toasted in a dry skillet
    over medium heat, for garnish
1 tablespoon fresh grapefruit zest for garnish

1. Bring water to a boil in a saucepan. Add the broccoli, cook for 2 minutes, and drain. Rinse in cold water, and drain again.
2. Combine the broccoli and mushrooms in a bowl and refrigerate until ready to serve.
3. Combine the grapefruit juice, rice vinegar, sugar, and Chinese hot oil in a small bowl.
4. About 30 minutes before serving, remove the broccoli and mushrooms from the refrigerator. Pour the grapefruit juice mixture over the broccoli and mushrooms, and toss well.
5. Place a lettuce leaf on each of four salad plates. Spoon portions of the broccoli salad onto each plate.
6. Sprinkle each salad with the pine nuts and grapefruit zest.

Broccoli Salad with Grapefruit Dressing

●

Makes 4 servings

• Curry powder was a late addition to Chinese cooking. This recipe is a good example of the way different cuisines adapt and learn from one another. For this recipe, we use more than our usual amount of oil in the wok because it becomes part of the salad dressing.

2 cups fresh corn kernels
1 stalk celery, chopped
2 large red bell peppers, seeds and ribs removed,
    and cut into $1/2$-inch cubes

SEASONINGS

1 tablespoon minced fresh ginger
1 tablespoon minced fresh garlic
1 to 2 teaspoons minced fresh green chili pepper

ADDITIONAL INGREDIENTS

2 tablespoons canola oil
1 tablespoon curry powder
$1/4$ cup rice vinegar
Salt to taste

PREPARATION

1. Bring water to a boil in a saucepan, add the corn kernels, and cook for 1 minute. Drain, place in a bowl, and set aside.
2. Place the celery and red bell peppers in separate bowls.
3. Combine the seasonings in a bowl.
4. Assemble your cooking tray.

Canola oil

Bowl of red bell peppers

Bowl of seasonings

Curry powder

Bowl of celery

COOKING

1. Heat a nonstick wok over high heat for 2 minutes.
2. Add the canola oil, then the seasonings, and stir-fry for 15 seconds.
3. Add the celery and stir-fry for 1 $^{1}/_{2}$ minutes.
4. Add the red bell pepper and stir-fry for 30 seconds.
5. Add the curry powder and mix well.
6. Transfer the red bell pepper mixture to a mixing bowl and add the corn.
7. Stir in the rice vinegar and salt to taste, and mix well.
8. Cover and refrigerate for at least 1 hour to allow the flavors to develop.

Spinach and Kiwi Salad

Makes 4 to 6 servings

- 4 kiwifruits
  1 tablespoon chopped fresh ginger
  1 tablespoon lemon juice
  1 tablespoon sesame oil
  1/2 cup orange juice
  1/2 tablespoon honey
  Salt and pepper to taste
  10 ounces fresh spinach, washed, tough stems removed,
      and torn into bite-sized pieces
  6 ounces fresh bean sprouts, rinsed

1. Peel the kiwifruits. Slice two into rounds and set aside for the garnish. Chop the remaining two kiwifruits.
2. Place the chopped kiwifruits, ginger, lemon juice, sesame oil, orange juice, honey, and salt and pepper to taste in the bowl of a food processor or blender, and pulse until the mixture is smooth. Set aside in a bowl in the refrigerator until ready to use.
3. Combine the spinach and bean sprouts in a large salad bowl. Pour the kiwi dressing over the spinach and bean sprouts and toss well.
4. Place portions of the salad on individual plates and arrange the kiwifruit rounds on top.

• Warm salads are newly popular—here is a Chinese version.

3 tablespoons lemon juice
2 tablespoons sesame oil
1 tablespoon sugar
1 teaspoon canola oil
1 teaspoon minced fresh garlic
4 large cucumbers, peeled, seeded, and cut into 2-inch julienne
Salt and pepper to taste
4 lettuce leaves, washed and dried
1 tablespoon sesame seeds, lightly browned in a dry skillet
    over medium heat, for garnish

1. Make the dressing by combining the lemon juice, sesame oil, and sugar in a small bowl. Stir well to dissolve the sugar. Set aside.
2. Heat a nonstick wok over high heat for 2 minutes.
3. Add the canola oil, then the garlic, and stir-fry for 15 seconds.
4. Add the cucumber and stir-fry for 1 minute.
5. Transfer the cucumber to a bowl and add the dressing. Toss to combine.
6. Season with salt and pepper to taste.
7. To serve, arrange a lettuce leaf on each of four salad plates. Spoon portions of the warm cucumbers over the lettuce and sprinkle with the sesame seeds.

Warm Cucumber Salad with Lemon-Sesame Dressing

•

Makes 4 servings

Cucumber

and

Mandarin

Orange

Salad

•

Makes 4
servings

• In the past, it would have been a rare Chinese salad that used anything but cooked or blanched and pickled ingredients. But in today's world, fresh salads like this one are increasingly popular.

1 medium cucumber, peeled, seeded, and cut into thin matchsticks
1 teaspoon salt
1/2 small head iceberg lettuce, shredded
3 scallions, both white and green parts, trimmed and thinly sliced
1 (11-ounce) can light (sugar-reduced) mandarin oranges, drained
1 cup orange juice, reduced to 1/2 cup by boiling for about 5 minutes
1 teaspoon low-sodium soy sauce
1 tablespoon rice vinegar
1/4 teaspoon hot red pepper sauce, such as Tabasco
1 tablespoon orange zest for garnish

1. Place the cucumber in a colander, sprinkle with the salt, and set aside for 20 minutes. Rinse in cold water and drain.
2. Combine the cucumber, lettuce, scallions, and mandarin oranges in a bowl.
3. Combine the orange juice, soy sauce, rice vinegar, and red pepper sauce in a small bowl and mix well.
4. Pour the orange juice dressing over the vegetables and fruit.
5. Serve on individual plates and garnish with the orange zest.

• The "creamy" dressing in this recipe is made with bean curd instead of cream, so it rates much better on the nutrition scales—and tastes better too.

CREAMY CUCUMBER DRESSING

1 teaspoon minced fresh garlic
1 teaspoon minced fresh ginger
1 teaspoon minced fresh green chili pepper
1 cucumber, peeled, seeded, and cut into chunks
8 ounces soft bean curd, drained
2 tablespoons rice vinegar
$^1/_2$ teaspoon salt

ADDITIONAL INGREDIENTS

2 cups salad greens, washed and torn into bite-sized pieces
1 mango, peeled and diced
$^1/_2$ cucumber, peeled, seeded, and diced
3 scallions, both white and green parts, chopped
2 tablespoons sesame seeds, lightly toasted in a dry skillet
    over medium heat, for garnish

1. Place the dressing ingredients in the bowl of a food processor and purée.
2. Arrange the greens on individual salad plates and place portions of the mango, cucumber, and scallion on top.
3. Spoon the dressing over the salad and sprinkle with the sesame seeds.

• Would you believe fruit salad with onion in it? Here the onion and curry powder give zip to the fresh fruits and balance their sweetness.

FRUIT MIXTURE

2 cups fresh pineapple, peeled, cored, and cut
    into 1-inch cubes
2 cups fresh melon, peeled, seeded, and cut into
    1-inch cubes
1 mango, peeled, pit removed, and cut into
    1-inch cubes
1/2 cup coarsely chopped red onion
1/2 cup chopped fresh mint

CURRIED CITRUS DRESSING

1/2 cup orange juice
1 tablespoon lemon juice
2 teaspoons low-sodium soy sauce
1 teaspoon minced fresh garlic
1 teaspoon minced fresh ginger
1 tablespoon sugar
1 teaspoon curry powder

ADDITIONAL INGREDIENTS

2 cups shredded savoy cabbage
1/2 cup pine nuts, lightly toasted in a dry skillet
    over medium heat, for garnish
6 sprigs fresh mint for garnish

1. Combine the fruit mixture ingredients in a large bowl and mix well.
2. Combine the curried citrus dressing ingredients in a small bowl and mix well.
3. Pour the dressing over the fruit and mix well.
4. Arrange a bed of savoy cabbage on each of 6 salad plates.
5. Spoon a portion of the fruit on top of the cabbage and garnish with the pine nuts and a sprig of mint.

Carrot-Pineapple Relish

Makes 4 servings

• This easy-to-make relish can be served as a side dish at dinner or with lettuce as a salad.

2 cups grated carrots
1 large green bell pepper, seeds and ribs removed, and finely chopped
1 (20-ounce) can drained unsweetened crushed pineapple
$1/2$ cup chopped water chestnuts
2 tablespoons rice vinegar
$1/4$ cup frozen pineapple juice concentrate
1 teaspoon minced fresh ginger

1. Combine the carrots, green bell pepper, pineapple, and water chestnuts in a bowl.
2. Combine the rice vinegar, pineapple juice concentrate, and ginger in a bowl and mix well.
3. Toss the rice vinegar dressing with the carrot mixture.
4. Refrigerate until ready to serve.

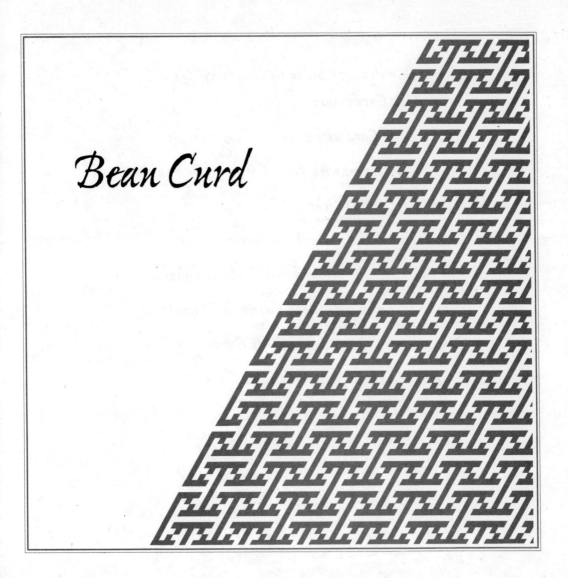

Bean Curd

RECESIPES

- Steamed Cauliflower Salad with Creamy "Gang Of Eight" Bean Curd Sauce

- Seared Bean Curd with Sesame-Ginger Sauce

- Crisp Green Beans with Bean Curd and Cashews

- Sweet and Sour Delight

- Crispy Bean Curd in Barbecue Sauce

- Bok Choy with Bean Curd and Red Radishes

- Eggplant Stuffed with Bean Curd and Peanuts

- Broccoli-Stem Hoisin with Bean Curd

- Fragrant Cabbage Stew with Bean Curd

• The "Gang of Eight" in this recipe is the eight flavoring ingredients that conspire to revolutionize the taste of mild-mannered cauliflower and bean curd.

SAUCE

8 ounces soft bean curd, drained
1 tablespoon minced fresh ginger
1 tablespoon minced fresh garlic
2 tablespoons minced fresh coriander leaves
1 teaspoon minced green chili pepper
$^1/_2$ teaspoon celery seed
1 tablespoon lemon juice
1 tablespoon brown sugar
1 teaspoon prepared mustard

ADDITIONAL INGREDIENTS

4 cups coarsely chopped fresh cauliflower
$^1/_2$ cup pine nuts, lightly browned in a dry skillet over medium heat

1. Combine the sauce ingredients in a food processor or blender and purée until smooth. Set aside.
2. Bring 3 to 4 inches of water to a boil in a wok.
3. Arrange the cauliflower on a plate in a bamboo steamer and cover. Place the steamer in the wok over the boiling water and steam for 3 to 4 minutes. The cauliflower should still be crisp.
4. Remove the cauliflower from the steamer, rinse in cold water to stop the cooking, and drain.
5. Toss the cauliflower with the bean curd sauce.
6. Stir in the pine nuts and chill in the refrigerator until ready to serve.

Steamed Cauliflower Salad with Creamy "Gang of Eight" Bean Curd Sauce

•

Makes 4 servings

Seared
Bean Curd
with
Sesame-
Ginger
Sauce

•

Makes 4
servings

• Here is one of the many ingenious Chinese ways to prepare bean curd.

1 pound firm bean curd
3 leeks
2 tablespoons minced fresh garlic
2 cups chopped onion

SAUCE

2 tablespoons low-sodium soy sauce
1 cup Vegetable Broth (page 49)
2 tablespoons dry sherry
1 tablespoon sesame oil

ADDITIONAL INGREDIENTS

Salt to taste
2 tablespoons canola oil
2 tablespoons sugar
2 tablespoons rice vinegar
1 tablespoon sesame seeds, lightly browned in a dry skillet over medium
    heat, for garnish

PREPARATION

1. Cut the bean curd into strips, 1 inch wide by 3 inches long. Place the bean
   curd strips in a single layer between several paper towels. Place a weight on
   top of the bean curd and set aside for about 20 minutes. This will remove
   any excess moisture.
2. Trim the root ends of the leeks. Cut off and discard the upper green parts,
   about 2 inches above each white bulb. Make a cross slit in the direction of

the bulb end in each leek. Rinse the leeks well under cold running water to remove any sand that has lodged in the layers. Slice the leeks into $1/2$-inch rings and place in a bowl.

3. Combine the garlic and onion in a bowl.
4. Combine the sauce ingredients in a small bowl.
5. Assemble your cooking tray.

ON YOUR TRAY

Canola oil	Bowl of leeks
Bean curd	Sugar
Salt	Rice vinegar
Bowl of garlic and onions	Bowl of sauce

COOKING

1. Preheat the oven to 225°.
2. Heat a nonstick wok over high heat for 2 minutes.
3. Add the canola oil, then the bean curd strips, and brown on all sides, about 1 minute each side. Sprinkle with salt to taste. Transfer to an ovenproof plate and keep in the warm oven.
4. Add the garlic and onion and stir-fry for about 2 minutes.
5. Add the leeks and stir-fry for 1 minute.
6. Add the sugar and stir-fry for 30 seconds to glaze.
7. Pour the rice vinegar over the onion mixture and stir.
8. Add the sauce and cook for 1 minute over high heat, stirring continuously.
9. Remove the bean curd from the oven and arrange on a serving platter.
10. Pour the sauce over the bean curd and sprinkle with the sesame seeds.

Crisp Green Beans with Bean Curd and Cashews

Makes 4 servings

• This dish is dry-cooked, meaning the sauce serves to flavor the beans but then cooks down to almost nothing so the beans end up "dry."

12 ounces young green beans, stems trimmed
4 ounces firm bean curd

SEASONINGS

1 tablespoon minced fresh garlic
1 teaspoon minced fresh ginger

SAUCE

2 tablespoons low-sodium soy sauce
1 tablespoon dry sherry
2 tablespoons water

ADDITIONAL INGREDIENTS

2 teaspoons canola oil
$^{1}/_{2}$ cup unsalted cashew pieces for garnish

PREPARATION

1. Bring water to a boil in a saucepan, add the green beans, and bring to a boil again. Cook, uncovered, for 3 minutes. Drain. Plunge the beans in a bowl of ice water to stop the cooking process. Drain again and place in a bowl.
2. Pat the bean curd dry with paper towels. Cut into $^{1}/_{2}$-inch cubes and place in a bowl.
3. Combine the seasonings in a small bowl.
4. Combine the sauce ingredients in a small bowl.
5. Assemble your cooking tray.

Canola oil   Bowl of sauce
Bowl of green beans   Bowl of bean curd
Bowl of seasonings

COOKING

1. Heat a nonstick wok over high heat for 2 minutes.
2. Add the canola oil, then the beans, and stir-fry for 1 minute.
3. Add the seasonings and the sauce, cover, and reduce the heat to medium.
   Cook for 5 minutes, stirring occasionally.
4. Remove the cover and gently stir in the bean curd.
5. Transfer to a serving platter and sprinkle with the cashews.

• The diverse ingredients in this dish make it a true vegetarian delight.

SEASONINGS

1 teaspoon minced fresh garlic
1 teaspoon minced fresh ginger
1/2 cup chopped onion

SAUCE

1/4 cup Vegetable Broth (page 49) or water
1/4 cup ketchup
1/4 cup rice vinegar
3 tablespoons sugar
2 tablespoons low-sodium soy sauce

ADDITIONAL INGREDIENTS

2 cups broccoli florets
2 peaches, peeled and cut into 1-inch chunks
1 cup canned or fresh pineapple chunks
1/2 cup whole chestnuts (available in cans) or water chestnuts
1 cup snow peas, strings and stems removed
1 teaspoon canola oil
4 ounces soft bean curd, drained and cut into 1-inch cubes

PREPARATION

1. Combine the seasonings in a small bowl.
2. Combine the sauce ingredients in a small bowl.

3. Bring water to a boil in a saucepan and boil the broccoli florets for 3 minutes. Drain and place in a bowl with the peaches, pineapple, and chestnuts.
4. Assemble your cooking tray.

ON YOUR TRAY

Canola oil
Bowl of seasonings
Bowl of snow peas
Bowl of broccoli, peaches,
    pineapple, and chestnuts

Bowl of sauce
Bowl of bean curd

COOKING

1. Heat a nonstick wok over high heat for 2 minutes.
2. Add the canola oil, then the seasonings, and stir-fry for 30 seconds.
3. Add the snow peas and stir-fry for 30 seconds.
4. Add the broccoli and fruit, then pour in the sauce. Stir to combine and heat through, about 2 minutes.
5. Gently stir in the bean curd.
6. Remove from the wok and serve.

Crispy Bean
Curd in
Barbecue
Sauce

•

Makes
4 servings

• Deep-frying is one of the traditional Chinese ways to prepare bean curd, so we wanted to include this recipe in our book. Here the bean curd has a lively sauce to give it spirit.

1 pound firm bean curd
$1/4$ cup flour

SEASONINGS

1 teaspoon minced fresh garlic
1 tablespoon minced fresh ginger
1 cup chopped onion

SAUCE

1 cup Vegetable Broth (page 49)
6 tablespoons ketchup
2 tablespoons low-sodium soy sauce
2 tablespoons dry sherry
2 tablespoons honey
1 teaspoon chili paste
1 teaspoon five-spice powder

ADDITIONAL INGREDIENTS

1 cup plus 1 teaspoon canola oil
1 cup chopped scallions, both white and green parts

PREPARATION

1. Cut the bean curd into strips 1 inch wide by 3 inches long.
2. Place the bean curd strips between several layers of paper towels and place a weight on top. Set aside for at least 30 minutes to remove excess moisture.

3. Roll the bean curd strips in the flour.
4. Combine the seasonings in a small bowl.
5. Combine the sauce ingredients in a small bowl.
6. Assemble your cooking tray for stir-frying.

ON YOUR TRAY

1 teaspoon canola oil   Bowl of sauce
Bowl of seasonings

COOKING

1. Pour 1 cup of the canola oil in a wok and heat to 375°. (Use a deep-frying
   thermometer to make sure the correct temperature is maintained.)
2. Cook the bean curd, a few pieces at a time, until it is crisp and brown, about
   1 minute. Be sure the oil comes back to 375° before frying the next batch.
   Keep the cooked bean curd warm in a low (225°) oven.
3. Heat a nonstick wok over high heat for 2 minutes.
4. Pour in 1 teaspoon of the canola oil, then add the seasonings, and stir-fry for
   30 seconds.
5. Add the sauce, cover, and reduce the heat to medium-low. Cook for 5 minutes, stirring occasionally.
6. Remove the warm bean curd from the oven and place it on a serving dish.
7. Add the scallions to the sauce, stir, then pour over the bean curd. Serve.

Bok Choy
with Bean
Curd and
Red
Radishes

•

*Makes 4
servings*

- 4 ounces firm bean curd
1 to 2 tablespoons flour
1/4 cup canola oil plus 1 teaspoon
1 pound bok choy, both white stems and green leaves,
    cut into 1-inch pieces
1 cup thinly sliced red radishes

SAUCE

1/2 cup Vegetable Broth (page 49)
1 tablespoon low-sodium soy sauce
1 tablespoon dry sherry

ADDITIONAL INGREDIENTS

1 teaspoon fresh minced ginger
1 tablespoon cornstarch dissolved in 2 tablespoons cold water

PREPARATION

1. Place the bean curd between several layers of paper towels and place a weight on top. Set aside for at least 30 minutes to remove excess moisture. Cut the bean curd into 1/2-inch cubes.
2. Coat each cube of bean curd with the flour.
3. Pour 1/4 cup of the canola oil in a wok and heat to 375°. (Use a deep-frying thermometer to make sure the correct temperature is maintained.) Fry the bean curd until lightly browned on all sides, about 1 minute. Drain on paper towels.
4. Combine the sauce ingredients.
5. Assemble your cooking tray.

1 teaspoon canola oil
Ginger
Bowl of bok choy
Bowl of red radishes

Bowl of sauce
Bowl of bean curd
Cornstarch mixture

COOKING

1. Heat a nonstick wok over high heat for 2 minutes.
2. Add the 1 teaspoon of canola oil, then the ginger, and stir-fry for 15 seconds.
3. Add the bok choy and stir-fry for 2 minutes.
4. Add the radishes, stir, pour in the sauce, and cover. Cook for 1 minute.
5. Remove the cover and gently stir in the bean curd.
6. Add the cornstarch mixture and stir until slightly thickened and glossy, about 30 seconds.
7. Remove from the wok and serve.

Eggplant
Stuffed with
Bean Curd
and Peanuts

•

Makes 4
servings

• Who but the Chinese could bring together this amazing combination of eggplant, bean curd, and peanuts and get it to taste good too?

1 medium eggplant
1 teaspoon salt

SEASONINGS

1 tablespoon minced fresh garlic
1 tablespoon minced fresh ginger
1/2 cup finely chopped onion

STUFFING

8 ounces soft bean curd, drained
1/2 cup whole wheat bread crumbs
3/4 cup peanuts
1 tablespoon low-sodium soy sauce
1 teaspoon sesame oil
3 tablespoons chopped fresh coriander leaves

ADDITIONAL INGREDIENTS

1/4 cup chopped scallions
1/4 cup chopped peanuts
2 teaspoons canola oil

PREPARATION

1. Cut the eggplant in half lengthwise. Scoop out the pulp, leaving a 1/2-inch shell. Coarsely chop the pulp and place in a strainer. Toss with the salt and set aside for 30 minutes. Rinse in cold water, drain, and place in a bowl.

2. To prepare the eggplant shells, preheat the oven to 400°. Place a rack in a roasting pan and pour in 1 inch of water. Place the shells, cut-side down, on the rack and cover tightly with foil. Bake for 15 minutes. Remove from the oven, and set aside until ready to fill.
3. Combine the seasonings in a bowl.
4. Place the stuffing ingredients in the bowl of a food processor and pulse until well blended, but leaving the nuts still chunky.
5. Combine the scallions and chopped peanuts in a bowl.
6. Assemble your cooking tray.

ON YOUR TRAY

Canola oil	Bowl of stuffing
Bowl of seasonings	Eggplant shells
Bowl of chopped eggplant	Bowl with scallions and peanuts

COOKING

1. Preheat the oven to 350°. Spray a roasting pan with canola oil spray.
2. Heat a nonstick wok over high heat for 2 minutes.
3. Add the canola oil, then the seasonings, and stir-fry for 30 seconds.
4. Add the chopped eggplant and stir-fry for 2 minutes.
5. Remove the eggplant from the wok and combine with the stuffing.
6. Spoon the eggplant mixture into the eggplant shells and sprinkle the scallions and peanuts over the top.
7. Place the stuffed eggplant shells in the roasting pan.
8. Bake uncovered for 25 to 30 minutes.

Broccoli-Stem Hoisin with Bean Curd

Makes 4 servings

• The Chinese are not a wasteful people. Here hoisin sauce and chili peppers give new life to broccoli stems and bean curd.

SEASONINGS

1 tablespoon minced fresh garlic
1 tablespoon minced fresh ginger
2 teaspoons minced fresh green chili peppers
1/2 cup chopped onion

SAUCE

2 tablespoons hoisin sauce
1 tablespoon low-sodium soy sauce

ADDITIONAL INGREDIENTS

8 broccoli stems, peeled and cut into 1/8-inch-wide by 2-inch-long julienne, or 3 cups broccoli slaw (see note)
8 ounces firm bean curd, cut into 3/4-inch cubes and patted dry with paper towels
2 teaspoons canola oil
2 tablespoons chopped scallions for garnish

PREPARATION

1. Combine the seasonings in a small bowl.
2. Combine the sauce ingredients in a small bowl.
3. Assemble your cooking tray.

Canola oil
Bowl of seasonings
Bowl of broccoli stems

Bowl of sauce
Bowl of bean curd

COOKING

1. Heat a nonstick wok over high heat for 2 minutes.
2. Add the canola oil, then the seasonings, and stir-fry for 30 seconds.
3. Add the broccoli stems and stir-fry for 2 $^{1}/_{2}$ minutes.
4. Add the sauce and stir to mix.
5. Gently fold in the bean curd and stir-fry just enough to heat through, about 30 seconds.
6. Remove from the wok and sprinkle with the scallions.

NOTE Broccoli slaw is available in plastic bags in supermarket produce sections.

• Star anise is the fragrant ingredient in this hearty casserole.

8 ounces firm bean curd
1 small head green cabbage, cut in quarters and cored
4 ounces fresh green beans, stems removed
3 medium carrots, peeled and cut into $1/2$-inch slices
1 cup dried Chinese mushrooms, soaked in hot water for 30 minutes
1 cup chopped onion

SEASONINGS

3 garlic cloves, peeled
3 slices fresh ginger, each about the size of a quarter
1 tablespoon star anise
3 to 4 dried red chili peppers, each about 2 inches long
1 (6-inch) square of cheesecloth

SAUCE

2 cups Vegetable Broth (page 49)
2 tablespoons dry sherry
2 tablespoons low-sodium soy sauce

PREPARATION

1. Place the bean curd between layers of paper towels to remove excess moisture. Cut into 1-inch cubes and set aside in a bowl, covered, until ready to add to the casserole.
2. Cut the cabbage into $1/2$-inch-wide shreds and place in a large, ovenproof covered casserole.
3. Cut the green beans into 2-inch lengths and add to the casserole.
4. Add the carrots to the casserole.

5. Drain the mushrooms, and remove and discard the stems. Add the caps to the casserole.
6. Add the onion to the casserole.
7. Put the seasonings on the cheesecloth square, pull up the corners and tie with a string to form a pouch like a bouquet garni. Add this to the casserole.
8. Combine the sauce ingredients. Pour the sauce into the casserole and cover.

COOKING

1. Preheat the oven to 350°.
2. Bake the casserole for 1 hour.
3. Remove from the oven and discard the pouch of seasonings.
4. Carefully stir in the bean curd.
5. Cover the casserole and return to the oven for an additional 15 minutes before serving.

Rice and
Noodle
Dishes

RECITES

- *Chinese-Style Boiled Rice*

- *Apricot-Almond Fried Rice*

- *Spinach Fried Brown Rice*

- *Orange Curried Fried Rice*

- *Broccoli and Pine Nut Fried Rice*

- *Sesame Noodles with Cucumbers and Red Radishes*

- *Summer Noodles*

- *Chow Fun Noodles*

- *Hot Pepper Rice Sticks with Peanuts*

- *Wontons with Red Pepper–Coriander Sauce*

- *Hoisin Noodles with Vegetables*

- The Chinese typically use long-grain rice. It cooks up to a fluffier, more granular consistency than short-grain rice, which tends to clump. For our Chinese cooking, we generally use a readily available long-grain brand such as Uncle Ben's or Carolina. You can also use brown rice if you wish and cook it the same way.

  It is very easy to make rice perfectly every time. Just follow this recipe.

2 cups long-grain white rice
3 cups cold water

1. Combine the rice and water in a 2-quart saucepan.
2. Place the saucepan over high heat. Cover and bring to a boil.
3. When steam begins to escape from under the lid, turn the heat to low and set your timer for 20 minutes. Do not remove the cover at any time, or the steam will escape. (The steam helps cook the rice.)
4. After 20 minutes, turn off the heat but allow the saucepan to rest another 20 minutes. Again, do not remove the cover.
5. Before serving, fluff the rice with a fork or chopsticks.

Chinese-Style Boiled Rice

•

Makes 4 to 6 servings (8 cups cooked rice)

• In traditional Chinese cooking, fried rice combinations are a way to use leftovers, including leftover boiled rice, so feel free to improvise.

1 cup coarsely chopped dried apricots
6 scallions, both white and green parts, chopped
4 cups Chinese-Style Boiled Rice (page 87)

SAUCE

$^1/_2$ cup Vegetable Broth (page 49)
1 tablespoon low-sodium soy sauce
1 teaspoon dry sherry

ADDITIONAL INGREDIENTS

1 tablespoon canola oil
2 teaspoons minced fresh garlic
$^1/_2$ cup sliced almonds, lightly browned in a dry skillet over medium heat,
    for garnish

PREPARATION

1. Combine the apricots and scallions in a bowl. Place the cooked rice in a bowl.
2. Combine the sauce ingredients in a small bowl.
3. Assemble your cooking tray.

ON YOUR TRAY

Canola oil   Bowl of cooked rice
Garlic   Bowl of sauce
Bowl of apricots and scallions

1. Heat a nonstick wok over high heat for 2 minutes.
2. Add the canola oil, then the garlic, and stir-fry for 15 seconds.
3. Add the apricots and scallions and stir.
4. Immediately add the rice and stir to break up any lumps.
5. Stir the sauce and pour over the rice. Stir to mix and heat through, 2 to 3 minutes.
6. Transfer to a serving bowl and sprinkle with the almonds.

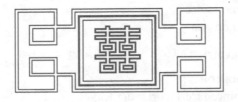

•

• The Chinese usually prefer white rice, but many vegetarians would rather eat brown rice. You can make this, and the other fried-rice recipes in this book, with either brown or white rice.

2 leeks
1 pound spinach, washed, tough stems removed, and coarsely chopped
3 cups brown Chinese-Style Boiled Rice (page 87)

SEASONINGS

1 tablespoon minced fresh ginger
1 tablespoon minced fresh garlic
1 cup chopped onion

SAUCE

2 tablespoons low-sodium soy sauce
1 tablespoon lemon juice
1 tablespoon lemon zest

ADDITIONAL INGREDIENTS

2 teaspoons canola oil
2 tablespoons minced fresh coriander leaves

PREPARATION

1. Trim the root ends of the leeks. Cut off and discard the upper green parts, about 2 inches above the white bulbs. Make a cross slit about 1 inch deep in the direction of the bulb end of each leek. Rinse the leeks well under cold running water to remove any sand that has lodged in the layers.

2. Place the leeks, spinach, and rice in separate bowls.
3. Combine the seasonings in a small bowl.
4. Combine the sauce ingredients in a small bowl.
5. Assemble your cooking tray.

ON YOUR TRAY

Canola oil
Bowl of seasonings
Bowl of leeks
Bowl of spinach

Bowl of rice
Bowl of sauce
Coriander

COOKING

1. Heat a nonstick wok over high heat for 2 minutes.
2. Add the canola oil, then the seasonings, and stir-fry for 30 seconds.
3. Add the leeks and stir-fry for 1 minute.
4. Add the spinach and stir-fry for 1 1/2 minutes.
5. Stir in the rice and stir-fry 1 minute to heat through.
6. Add the sauce and stir to combine.
7. Add the coriander and stir. Remove from the wok and serve.

*Orange
Curried
Fried
Rice*

•

*Makes 4
servings*

SEASONINGS

1 tablespoon minced fresh ginger
1 teaspoon minced fresh garlic
$^1/_2$ cup chopped onion
1 tablespoon curry powder

VEGETABLES

1 cup chopped scallions, both white and green parts
$^1/_2$ cup grated carrots
$^1/_4$ cup chopped water chestnuts
1 tablespoon orange zest

SAUCE

2 tablespoons frozen orange juice concentrate
1 tablespoon low-sodium soy sauce
1 tablespoon dry sherry

ADDITIONAL INGREDIENTS

4 cups Chinese-Style Boiled Rice (page 87)
2 teaspoons canola oil

PREPARATION

1. Combine the seasonings in a small bowl.
2. Combine the vegetables in a bowl.
3. Combine the sauce ingredients in a small bowl.
4. Assemble your cooking tray.

Canola oil

Bowl of seasonings

Bowl of vegetables

Bowl of sauce

Bowl of rice

COOKING

1. Heat a nonstick wok over high heat for 2 minutes.
2. Add the canola oil, then the seasonings, and stir-fry for 30 seconds.
3. Add the vegetables and stir-fry for 30 seconds.
4. Pour in the sauce, then add the rice, and stir to mix.
5. Stir-fry for about 1 minute to heat the rice through.
6. Remove from the wok and serve.

Broccoli
and
Pine Nut
Fried Rice

*

*Makes 4
servings*

- SEASONINGS
  1 tablespoon minced fresh garlic
  1 tablespoon minced fresh ginger
  $^{1}/_{2}$ cup chopped onion

SAUCE

$^{1}/_{2}$ cup Vegetable Broth (page 49) or water
2 tablespoons low-sodium soy sauce
2 tablespoons dry sherry

ADDITIONAL INGREDIENTS

$^{1}/_{2}$ cup chopped fresh parsley
$^{1}/_{4}$ cup pine nuts, lightly browned in a dry skillet over medium heat
2 teaspoons canola oil
2 cups coarsely chopped broccoli florets
3 cups cooked Chinese-Style Boiled Rice (page 87)

PREPARATION

1. Combine the seasonings in a small bowl.
2. Combine the sauce ingredients in a small bowl.
3. Combine the parsley and pine nuts in a small bowl.
4. Assemble your cooking tray.

ON YOUR TRAY

Canola oil
Bowl of seasonings
Bowl of broccoli

Bowl of sauce
Bowl of rice
Bowl of parsley and pine nuts

COOKING

1. Heat a nonstick wok over high heat for 2 minutes.
2. Add the canola oil, then the seasonings, and stir-fry for 15 seconds.
3. Add the broccoli and stir-fry for 1 minute.
4. Pour in the sauce, cover, and turn heat to low. Cook for 2 minutes.
5. Remove the cover and return the heat to high. Add the rice and stir to break up any lumps.
6. Add the parsley and pine nuts and toss to mix well.
7. Stir-fry for about 1 minute to heat the rice through.

Sesame
Noodles
with
Cucumbers
and Red
Radishes

•

Makes 4
servings

• Sesame noodles come in many different versions; this one has radishes as a surprise ingredient.

1 pound fresh Chinese egg noodles or fettucine

SAUCE
1 tablespoon minced fresh ginger
1 teaspoon minced fresh garlic
1 teaspoon minced fresh green chili pepper
$1/4$ cup low-sodium soy sauce
$1/4$ cup rice vinegar
$3/4$ cup reduced-fat peanut butter
2 tablespoons honey
2 tablespoons sesame oil
$1/2$ teaspoon Chinese hot oil

ADDITIONAL INGREDIENTS

2 cucumbers, peeled, seeded, and cut into thin slivers
8 red radishes, thinly sliced
$1/2$ cup chopped scallions, both white and green parts
2 tablespoons sesame seeds, lightly toasted in a dry skillet
    over medium heat, for garnish

1. Bring 4 to 6 quarts of water to a boil and cook the noodles for 3 minutes.
2. Meanwhile, combine the sauce ingredients in the bowl of a food processor and blend until smooth.
3. Drain the noodles and toss with the sauce.
4. Toss in the cucumbers and radishes.

5. Arrange on a serving platter and sprinkle the scallions and sesame seeds over the top.
6. Serve hot or at room temperature. If you plan to serve the noodles at room temperature, toss them with a little water before serving if they seem too sticky.

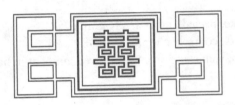

● Why "summer" noodles? Because once vegetables were available only in their local growing season. Now, of course, vegetables like the ones in this noodle dish are easy to find year-round.

8 ounces fresh Chinese egg noodles
1/4 cup Vegetable Broth (page 49) or water

SEASONINGS

1 teaspoon minced fresh garlic
1 tablespoon minced fresh ginger
1 cup finely chopped onion

VEGETABLES

2 medium carrots, peeled and coarsely grated
8 water chestnuts, coarsely chopped
1 cup snow peas, stems and strings removed, and cut in half

SAUCE

1/2 cup Vegetable Broth (page 49) or water
3 tablespoons low-sodium soy sauce
1/2 teaspoon dried crushed red pepper

ADDITIONAL INGREDIENT

2 teaspoons canola oil

PREPARATION

1. Boil the noodles for 3 minutes, drain, and place in a bowl with the ¹/4 cup vegetable broth.
2. Combine the seasonings in a small bowl.
3. Combine the carrots and water chestnuts in a bowl. Place the snow peas in a separate bowl.
4. Combine the sauce ingredients in a small bowl.
5. Assemble your cooking tray.

ON YOUR TRAY

Canola oil
Bowl of seasonings
Bowl of carrots and water chestnuts

Bowl of sauce
Bowl of snow peas
Bowl of noodles

COOKING

1. Heat a nonstick wok over high heat for 2 minutes. Add the canola oil, then the seasonings, and stir-fry for 15 seconds.
2. Add the carrots and water chestnuts and stir.
3. Add the sauce, cover, and simmer for 2 minutes.
4. Remove the cover, add the snow peas, and stir.
5. Add the noodles and toss until heated through and the vegetables are incorporated, about 2 minutes.
6. Remove from the wok and serve.

• The rice noodles used in this recipe are fresh and come in sheets that you need to cut at home into wide noodles. These noodles differ from the dried rice noodles called "rice sticks" that are also found in Asian markets. If you can't find rice noodles in sheets, substitute fettuccine. You don't have to precook rice noodles; but if you use fettuccine, cook it first according to package directions.

6 dried Chinese mushrooms, soaked in hot water
    for 30 minutes
1 cup broccoli florets
1 cup shredded cabbage
1 large red bell pepper, seeds and ribs removed, and
    cut into thin shreds

SEASONINGS

1 tablespoon minced fresh garlic
1 tablespoon minced fresh ginger
2 teaspoons minced fresh green chili pepper

SAUCE

1 cup Vegetable Broth (page 49)
2 tablespoons low-sodium soy sauce
2 tablespoons dry sherry
1 teaspoon sugar

ADDITIONAL INGREDIENTS

1 tablespoon canola oil
1 pound fresh rice noodle sheets, cut $1/2$ inch wide

PREPARATION

1. Remove the mushroom stems and discard them. Cut the caps into $1/8$-inch slices. Place the mushroom slices in a bowl. Add the broccoli florets to the same bowl.
2. Place the cabbage and red bell pepper in separate bowls.
3. Combine the seasonings in a small bowl.
4. Combine the sauce ingredients in a bowl.
5. Assemble your cooking tray.

ON YOUR TRAY

Canola oil

Bowl of sauce

Bowl of seasonings

Bowl of red pepper

Bowl of cabbage

Bowl of noodles

Bowl of broccoli and mushrooms

COOKING

1. Heat a nonstick wok over high heat for 2 minutes.
2. Add the canola oil, then the seasonings, and stir-fry for 15 seconds.
3. Add the cabbage and stir-fry for 2 minutes.
4. Add the broccoli and mushrooms and stir-fry for 30 seconds.
5. Pour in the sauce, cover, and lower the heat. Cook for 3 minutes.
6. Remove the cover and return to high heat. Add the red peppers and stir.
7. Add the noodles, and toss with the vegetables to heat through, about 2 minutes.

Hot

Pepper

Rice

Sticks

with

Peanuts

•

Makes 4
servings

• Rice sticks are very thin dried rice noodles sold in Asian markets and other specialty food stores. If you can't find them, substitute vermicelli.

8 ounces dried Chinese rice sticks

SAUCE

2 tablespoons low-sodium soy sauce
1 tablespoon rice vinegar
1 tablespoon chili paste
1/4 cup Vegetable Broth (page 49) or water
1 tablespoon sesame oil

SEASONINGS

1 tablespoon minced fresh garlic
1 tablespoon minced fresh ginger
1/2 cup chopped onion

ADDITIONAL INGREDIENTS

1/2 red bell pepper, seeds and ribs removed
1/2 green bell pepper, seeds and ribs removed
4 scallions
1 bunch watercress, washed and tough stems removed
2 teaspoons canola oil
1/2 cup chopped peanuts for garnish

PREPARATION

1. Bring 4 quarts of water to a boil in a pot, add the rice sticks, and remove the pot from the burner. Set aside uncovered for 10 minutes to soften the noodles, then drain and place in a bowl.

2. Combine the sauce ingredients and pour over the noodles. Toss well.
3. Combine the seasonings in a small bowl.
4. Cut the red and green peppers into 3-inch-long shreds and place in a bowl.
5. Cut the scallions into 3-inch-long shreds (both the white and green parts) and place in a bowl.
6. Bring water to a boil in a small saucepan, add the watercress, stir, then drain and rinse in cold water. Drain, then coarsely chop the watercress and place in a bowl.
7. Assemble your cooking tray.

ON YOUR TRAY

Canola oil
Bowl of seasonings
Bowl of peppers

Bowl of scallions
Bowl of watercress
Bowl of noodles with sauce

COOKING

1. Heat a nonstick wok over high heat for 2 minutes.
2. Add the canola oil, then the seasonings, and stir-fry for 30 seconds.
3. Add the peppers and stir-fry for 1 minute.
4. Add the scallions and stir-fry for 30 seconds.
5. Add the watercress and stir-fry for 30 seconds.
6. Add the noodles and toss to mix with the vegetables. Cook until heated through, about 1 minute.
7. Transfer to a serving platter and sprinkle with the peanuts.

*Wontons
with Red
Pepper–
Coriander
Sauce*

•

Makes 4
servings

• This lively sauce gives wontons a new dimension. To make the wontons, follow the instructions for vegetable-filled wontons (pages 30–31). But don't deep-
fry them; here they are boiled.

This sauce is also delicious over Chinese egg noodles.

3 large red bell peppers, seeds and ribs removed

SEASONINGS

1 tablespoon minced fresh garlic
1 teaspoon minced fresh ginger
1/2 cup chopped onion

SAUCE

3 cups Vegetable Broth (page 49)
1 (8-ounce) can tomato sauce
2 tablespoons low-sodium soy sauce
1 tablespoon dry sherry
1 tablespoon chili paste
1/4 cup minced fresh coriander leaves

ADDITIONAL INGREDIENTS

36 uncooked vegetable-filled wontons (pages 30–31)
2 teaspoons canola oil
2 tablespoons cornstarch dissolved in 3 tablespoons cold water
2 scallions, both white and green parts, finely chopped for garnish

PREPARATION

1. Cut the red peppers into 1-inch squares.
2. Combine the seasonings in a small bowl.
3. Combine the sauce ingredients in a bowl.
4. Assemble your cooking tray.
5. Bring several quarts of water to a boil. Add the wontons and bring the water back to a boil. Turn the heat to medium and gently cook for 5 to 6 minutes. Drain and keep warm while preparing the sauce.

ON YOUR TRAY

Canola oil

Bowl of seasonings

Bowl of red pepper

Bowl of sauce

Cornstarch mixture

COOKING

1. Heat a nonstick wok over high heat for 2 minutes.
2. Add the canola oil, then the seasonings, and stir-fry for 30 seconds.
3. Add the red pepper and stir-fry for 30 seconds.
4. Add the sauce, cover, and turn the heat to medium. Cook for 5 minutes.
5. Remove the cover and add the cornstarch mixture. Stir until the sauce is thickened, about 30 seconds.
6. Pour sauce over the cooked wontons. Garnish with the scallions.

Hoisin

Noodles

with

Vegetables

•

*Makes 4
servings*

• Noodles are a traditional birthday food in China because their length symbolizes a long life. But noodle dishes are popular throughout the year and throughout the country, as a snack, a side dish, or a main dish. This hearty noodle and vegetable concoction makes an excellent vegetarian main dish. Hoisin sauce is the predominant flavor, but the green chili pepper adds a bit of zip.

8 ounces fresh Chinese egg noodles
1/4 cup Vegetable Broth (page 49) or water

SEASONINGS

1/2 cup chopped onion
1 tablespoon minced fresh ginger
1 tablespoon minced fresh garlic
1 tablespoon minced fresh green chili pepper

VEGETABLES

2 cups shredded green cabbage
1 red bell pepper, seeds and ribs removed
2 cups shredded radicchio
2 cups broccoli florets

SAUCE

1/2 cup Vegetable Broth (page 49)
2 tablespoons rice vinegar
2 tablespoons low-sodium soy sauce

ADDITIONAL INGREDIENTS

1/4 cup hoisin sauce
1 tablespoon canola oil
1 tablespoon sesame oil
1/2 cup chopped scallions for garnish

PREPARATION

1. Boil the noodles for 3 minutes, drain them and put in a bowl with the
   1/4 cup vegetable broth.
2. Combine the seasonings in a small bowl.
3. Place the green cabbage in a bowl.
4. Cut the red bell pepper into 1-inch squares and combine with the radicchio
   in a bowl.
5. Blanch the broccoli florets for 5 minutes, drain, and rinse in cold water to
   stop the cooking. Place the cooked broccoli florets in a bowl.
6. Combine the sauce ingredients in a bowl.
7. Assemble your cooking tray.

ON YOUR TRAY

Canola oil
Bowl of seasonings
Bowl of cabbage
Bowl of red pepper and radicchio
Bowl of noodles

Bowl of sauce
Bowl of broccoli
Hoisin sauce
Sesame oil

(continues)

1. Heat a nonstick wok over high heat for 2 minutes.
2. Add the canola oil, then the seasonings, and stir-fry for 15 seconds.
3. Add the cabbage and stir-fry for 3 minutes.
4. Add the red pepper and radicchio and stir-fry for 1 minute.
5. Add the noodles and toss to mix.
6. Add the sauce and toss to mix.
7. Add the broccoli and mix well, cooking for 1 minute.
8. Stir in the hoisin sauce.
9. Sprinkle the sesame oil over the noodles.
10. Transfer to a serving platter. Sprinkle with the scallions and serve.

Vegetable Entrées and Side Dishes

RECIPES

- *Steamed Vegetables with Watercress and Coriander Sauce*
- *Hot and Sour Vegetables*
- *Hoisin Green Beans and Peppers*
- *Stir-Fried Asparagus and Baby Corn*
- *Spicy Swiss Chard and Tangerines*
- *Spinach, Tomato, and Water Chestnuts*
- *Glazed Pineapple, Carrots, and Sweet Potato*
- *Wok-Seared Baby Bok Choy with Caramelized Onion*
- *Glazed Sweet and Sour Leeks*
- *Stir-Fried Sweet Peppers and Snow Peas*
- *Stir-Fried Snow Peas, Anise, and Cucumbers*
- *Honey-Glazed Brussels Sprouts with Red Pepper*
- *Sugar Snaps and Shiitakes in Lemon-Garlic Sauce*
- *Triple Onion Bake*

- Roasted Eggplant, Anise, and Sweet Onions
- Stir-Fried Broccoli and Red Pepper
- Curried Vegetable Pie
- Stir-Fried Asparagus, Golden Peppers, and Water Chestnuts
- Spaghetti Squash with Spinach
- Steamed Broccoli and Water Chestnuts in Black Bean Sauce

Steamed
Vegetables
with
Watercress
and
Coriander
Sauce

•

Makes 4
servings

• In this recipe, the more delicate ingredients, mushrooms and peas, are added in a separate step near the end of the steaming cycle. This is typical of Chinese recipes—each ingredient is cooked only as long as needed to cook through.

1 leek
1 small sweet potato, peeled and cut into $1/4$-inch cubes
1 purple turnip, peeled and cut into $1/4$-inch cubes
1 cup coarsely chopped green cabbage
1 cup sliced fresh mushrooms
1 cup frozen green peas, thawed

SEASONINGS

1 tablespoon low-sodium soy sauce
1 tablespoon dry sherry

SAUCE

$1/2$ cup finely chopped watercress (tough stems removed)
2 tablespoons finely chopped fresh coriander leaves
1 tablespoon minced fresh ginger
1 tablespoon minced fresh garlic
$1/4$ cup finely chopped onion
2 tablespoons water
2 teaspoons hoisin sauce

PREPARATION

1. Trim the root end of the leek. Cut off and discard the upper green part, about 2 inches above the white bulb. Make a cross slit about 1 inch deep in the direction of the bulb end. Rinse the leek well under cold running water to remove any sand that has lodged in the layers. Coarsely chop the leek.
2. Combine the potato, turnip, cabbage, and leek in a heatproof bowl.
3. Combine the mushrooms and peas in a separate small bowl.
4. Combine the seasonings and sprinkle over the vegetables in the heatproof bowl.
5. Combine the sauce ingredients in a blender or the bowl of a food processor and blend until smooth. Place in a bowl.

COOKING

1. Bring 3 to 4 inches of water to a boil in the wok. (Check from time to time during the cooking to see if you need to add more boiling water to the wok. Keep a kettle with simmering water on the stove, just in case.)
2. Place the heatproof bowl of vegetables and seasonings on the rack of a bamboo steamer and cover.
3. Place the covered steamer in the wok over the boiling water and steam for 12 minutes.
4. Carefully remove the steamer cover and add the mushrooms and peas to the rest of the vegetables. Cover and continue steaming for 3 minutes more.
5. Remove the steamer from the wok and let cool a few minutes before removing the lid.
6. Transfer the vegetables to a bowl. Stir in the sauce and serve.

Hot and Sour Vegetables

Makes 4
servings

● The hot (chili paste) and sour (rice vinegar) taste combination is always popular with fans of Chinese food. With just one tablespoon of chili paste, this version is only mildly hot.

VEGETABLES

2 cups green cabbage, thinly sliced and separated into strips
    2 to 3 inches long
1 cup sliced fresh mushrooms
$1/2$ green bell pepper, seeds and ribs removed, and cut into
    $1/2$-inch squares
$1/2$ red bell pepper, seeds and ribs removed, and cut into
    $1/2$-inch squares

SEASONINGS

1 teaspoon minced fresh garlic
1 tablespoon minced fresh ginger
2 scallions, both white and green parts, chopped

SAUCE

$1/2$ cup Vegetable Broth (page 49) or water
1 tablespoon low-sodium soy sauce
2 tablespoons rice vinegar
1 tablespoon chili paste
1 teaspoon sugar

ADDITIONAL INGREDIENTS

2 teaspoons canola oil
1 tablespoon sesame seeds, lightly toasted in a dry skillet
    over medium heat, for garnish

PREPARATION

1. Combine the vegetables in a bowl.
2. Combine the seasonings in a small bowl.
3. Combine the sauce ingredients in a bowl.
4. Assemble your cooking tray.

ON YOUR TRAY

Canola oil	Bowl of vegetables
Bowl of seasonings	Bowl of sauce

COOKING

1. Heat a nonstick wok over high heat for 2 minutes.
2. Add the canola oil, then the seasonings and stir-fry for 15 seconds.
3. Add the vegetables and stir-fry for 1 minute.
4. Add the sauce, stir, and cover. Reduce the heat to medium and cook for 3 minutes.
5. Remove the cover, return to high heat, and stir-fry for 1 minute more.
6. Arrange the vegetables on a platter, sprinkle with the sesame seeds, and serve.

•

• 8 ounces small green beans, stems trimmed
2 medium green bell peppers, seeds and ribs removed, coarsely chopped

SEASONINGS

1 teaspoon minced fresh garlic
1 teaspoon minced fresh ginger
2 scallions, both white and green parts, chopped

ADDITIONAL INGREDIENTS

1 cup Vegetable Broth (page 49)
1 tablespoon low-sodium soy sauce
2 tablespoons hoisin sauce
1 teaspoon chili paste
2 teaspoons canola oil
2 teaspoons cornstarch dissolved in 1 tablespoon cold water

PREPARATION

1. Place the green beans and green peppers in separate bowls.
2. Combine the seasonings in a small bowl.
3. Combine the vegetable broth and soy sauce in one bowl and the hoisin sauce and chili paste in another.
4. Assemble your cooking tray.

ON YOUR TRAY

Canola oil
Bowl of seasonings
Bowl of green peppers
Bowl of green beans

Bowl of vegetable broth and soy
  sauce
Bowl of hoisin sauce and chili paste
Cornstarch mixture

1. Heat a nonstick wok over high heat for 2 minutes.
2. Add the canola oil, then the seasonings, and stir-fry for 15 seconds.
3. Add the green peppers and stir-fry for 30 seconds.
4. Add the green beans and stir-fry for 30 seconds.
5. Pour in the vegetable broth mixture, cover, reduce the heat to low and cook for 5 minutes.
6. Remove the cover and stir in the hoisin mixture.
7. If the sauce seems too thin, add the cornstarch mixture and stir until thickened.
8. Remove from the wok and serve.

Stir-Fried Asparagus and Baby Corn

Makes 4 servings

- 1 pound fresh asparagus, trimmed and cut into 2-inch lengths
- 8 ears canned baby corn, drained and cut in half lengthwise
- 1/2 cup drained canned straw mushrooms

SAUCE

1/2 cup Vegetable Broth (page 49)
1 tablespoon low-sodium soy sauce
1 tablespoon dry sherry

ADDITIONAL INGREDIENTS

2 teaspoons canola oil
1 tablespoon minced fresh garlic

PREPARATION

1. Put the asparagus in a bowl.
2. Combine the corn and mushrooms in a separate bowl.
3. Combine the sauce ingredients in a small bowl.
4. Assemble your cooking tray.

ON YOUR TRAY

Canola oil
Garlic
Bowl of asparagus

Bowl of sauce
Bowl of corn and mushrooms

COOKING

1. Heat a nonstick wok over high heat for 2 minutes.
2. Add the canola oil, then the garlic, and stir-fry for 15 seconds.
3. Add the asparagus and stir-fry for 30 seconds.
4. Add the sauce, cover, reduce the heat to medium and cook for 3 minutes.
5. Remove the cover, return to high heat, and stir in the corn and mushrooms. Cook for 1 minute to heat through.
6. Remove from the wok and serve.

• This is a good example of the Chinese inclination to bring together contrasting tastes and colors. Here, strong-flavored green Swiss chard, subtly flavored orange tangerines, and red hot chili peppers get along with each other surprisingly well.

2 pounds Swiss chard

SEASONINGS

1 tablespoon minced fresh garlic
3 dried red chili peppers, each about 2 inches long
2 tablespoons minced tangerine zest

SAUCE

3 tablespoons frozen tangerine or orange juice concentrate
1 tablespoon low-sodium soy sauce
1 tablespoon dry sherry

ADDITIONAL INGREDIENTS

1 large tangerine, peeled and separated into segments
1 teaspoon canola oil
2 teaspoons cornstarch dissolved in 1 tablespoon cold water

PREPARATION

1. Remove and discard the Swiss chard stems. Wash the leaves thoroughly to remove any sand clinging to them. Coarsely chop the leaves and place in a bowl.
2. Combine the seasonings in a small bowl.

3. Combine the sauce ingredients in a small bowl.
4. Remove the seeds from the tangerine segments.
5. Assemble your cooking tray.

Canola oil	Bowl of sauce
Bowl of seasonings	Tangerine segments
Bowl of Swiss chard	Cornstarch mixture

COOKING

1. Heat a nonstick wok over high heat for 2 minutes.
2. Add the canola oil, then the seasonings, and stir-fry for 30 seconds.
3. Add the Swiss chard and stir until wilted, about 30 seconds.
4. Add the sauce, cover, and reduce the heat to medium. Cook for 5 minutes.
5. Remove the cover and add the tangerine segments. Stir until heated through, about 1 minute.
6. If the sauce is too thin, stir in the cornstarch mixture until slightly thickened.
7. Remove chili peppers before serving.

Spinach, Tomato, and Water Chestnuts

Makes 4 servings

- 1 1/2 pounds fresh spinach, washed and tough stems removed
  1 large ripe tomato, cut into 1/2-inch cubes
  8 water chestnuts, sliced

SEASONINGS

1 cup coarsely chopped onion
1 teaspoon minced fresh ginger
1 teaspoon minced fresh garlic

ADDITIONAL INGREDIENTS

1 teaspoon canola oil
1/2 teaspoon salt

PREPARATION

1. Place the spinach, tomato, and water chestnuts in separate bowls.
2. Combine the seasonings in a small bowl.
3. Assemble your cooking tray.

ON YOUR TRAY

Canola oil
Bowl of seasonings
Bowl of spinach

Bowl of tomato
Bowl of water chestnuts
Salt

COOKING

1. Heat a nonstick wok over high heat for 2 minutes.
2. Add the canola oil, then the seasonings, and stir-fry for 1 minute.
3. Add the spinach and cover. Reduce the heat to medium and cook for 1 minute.
4. Remove the cover, add the tomato, then the water chestnuts and salt. Stir-fry for 1 minute.
5. Remove from the wok and serve.

Glazed Pineapple, Carrots, and Sweet Potato

Serves 4

SAUCE

Drained pineapple juice from canned pineapple (see below)
    plus enough orange juice to make 1 cup
1 teaspoon curry powder
1 tablespoon minced fresh ginger
1 tablespoon low-sodium soy sauce

ADDITIONAL INGREDIENTS

4 carrots, peeled and sliced into $1/8$-inch rounds
2 sweet potatoes, peeled and cut into $1/2$-inch cubes
$1/2$ cup canned crushed pineapple, drained and juice reserved

PREPARATION

1. Combine the sauce ingredients in a small bowl.
2. Assemble your cooking tray.

ON YOUR TRAY

Bowl of sauce   Bowl of sweet potatoes
Bowl of carrots   Bowl of pineapple

COOKING

1. Bring the sauce ingredients to a boil in a wok. Add the carrots, cover, and cook for 3 minutes.
2. Add the sweet potatoes, cover, and cook for 3 more minutes.
3. Stir in the crushed pineapple, cover, and cook for 1 minute.
4. Remove from the wok and serve.

• Wok-searing differs from stir-frying because the ingredient is not tossed and turned but is left to brown and sear on just one side. This recipe combines searing and stir-frying.

1 tablespoon plus 1 teaspoon canola oil
5 heads small bok choy, cut in half lengthwise (about 10 ounces)
1/2 cup chopped onion
2 teaspoons sugar
1 cup Vegetable Broth (page 49)
Salt to taste

1. Heat a nonstick wok over high heat for 2 minutes.
2. Add 1 tablespoon of the canola oil and arrange the bok choy cut-side down on the hot wok surface. Sear for 1 1/2 to 2 minutes, or until the cut surface is quite brown. Transfer to a platter.
3. Add the remaining 1 teaspoon of the canola oil to the wok and add the onions. Stir-fry for 2 minutes, until the onions are dark brown.
4. Sprinkle the sugar over the onions and stir-fry for 30 seconds to caramelize the sugar.
5. Add the broth, cover, and reduce the heat to low. Cook for 2 minutes.
6. Remove the cover and pour the onions and sauce over the bok choy. Season with salt if desired.

Glazed Sweet and Sour Leeks

•

Makes 4 servings

• This dish can be served warm or cold to go with a main dish salad, soup, or sandwich.

8 leeks, each about 1 inch wide
3 slices ginger, each about the size of a quarter
1 cup Vegetable Broth (page 49)
4 dried red chili peppers, each about 1 1/2 to 2 inches long
1/2 teaspoon fennel seeds
2 teaspoons sesame seeds

SAUCE

1/2 cup broth reserved after cooking the leeks
2 tablespoons sugar
1/4 cup rice vinegar
2 teaspoons sesame oil

ADDITIONAL INGREDIENT

2 teaspoons canola oil

PREPARATION

1. Trim the root end of each leek. Cut off and discard the upper green parts, about 2 inches above the white bulbs. Make a cross slit about 1 inch deep in the direction of the bulb end of each leek. Rinse well under cold running water to remove any sand that has lodged in the layers.
2. Combine the leeks, ginger, and broth in a saucepan and bring to a boil. Cover and cook over low heat for 5 to 6 minutes, or until leeks are fork-tender. Drain and reserve the cooking liquid. Set aside.

3. Combine the sauce ingredients in a bowl.
4. Place the chili peppers in one bowl, and the fennel seeds and sesame seeds in another.
5. Assemble your cooking tray.

ON YOUR TRAY

Canola oil
Dried chili peppers
Fennel seeds and sesame seeds

Bowl of sauce
Cooked leeks

COOKING

1. Heat a nonstick wok over high heat for 2 minutes.
2. Add the canola oil, then the chili peppers, and stir-fry for 15 seconds.
3. Add the fennel seeds and sesame seeds and stir-fry for 10 seconds.
4. Pour in the sauce and cook for 30 seconds.
5. Add the cooked leeks and turn them in the sauce to coat. Cook until the leeks are glazed and the sauce has reduced, about 45 seconds.
6. Remove and discard the chili peppers. Transfer to a serving platter, or cover and refrigerate several hours until ready to serve.

Stir-Fried
Sweet
Peppers
and Snow
Peas

•

Makes 4
servings

• 1 red bell pepper, seeds and ribs removed, and cut into 1-inch squares
  1 orange bell pepper, seeds and ribs removed, and cut into 1-inch squares
  8 ounces snow peas, stems and strings removed
  1 cup fresh bean sprouts

SEASONINGS

1/2 cup chopped onion
1 tablespoon minced fresh garlic
1 tablespoon minced fresh ginger

SAUCE

1/2 cup Vegetable Broth (page 49) or water
1 tablespoon low-sodium soy sauce

ADDITIONAL INGREDIENTS

2 teaspoons canola oil
1 teaspoon cornstarch dissolved in 2 teaspoons cold water

PREPARATION

1. Combine the red and orange peppers in a bowl.
2. Combine the snow peas and bean sprouts in a bowl. If any snow peas are especially long, cut them in half on the diagonal.
3. Combine the seasonings in a bowl.
4. Combine the sauce ingredients in a small bowl.
5. Assemble your cooking tray.

Canola oil

Bowl of seasonings

Bowl of red and orange peppers

Bowl of snow peas and bean sprouts

Bowl of sauce

Cornstarch mixture

COOKING

1. Heat a nonstick wok over high heat for 2 minutes.
2. Add the canola oil, then the seasonings, and stir-fry for 15 seconds.
3. Add the red and orange peppers and stir-fry for 2 minutes.
4. Add the snow peas and bean sprouts and stir-fry for 1 minute.
5. Add the sauce and stir.
6. Add the cornstarch mixture and stir until thickened, about 30 seconds.
7. Remove from the wok and serve.

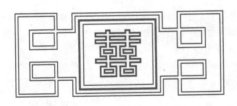

Stir-Fried Snow Peas, Anise, and Cucumbers

Makes 4 servings

- 3 medium cucumbers, peeled
- 6 ounces fresh snow peas, strings and stems removed
- 1 fresh anise bulb (fennel), cut into $1/8$-inch slivers

SAUCE

$1/2$ cup Vegetable Broth (page 49) or water
1 tablespoon dry sherry
1 tablespoon low-sodium soy sauce

ADDITIONAL INGREDIENTS

2 teaspoons canola oil
1 tablespoon minced fresh garlic
1 teaspoon cornstarch dissolved in 2 teaspoons cold water
2 tablespoons chopped fresh anise leaves for garnish

PREPARATION

1. Cut the cucumbers in half lengthwise, remove the seeds, and cut into $1/4$-inch slices.
2. Place the cucumbers, snow peas, and anise in separate bowls.
3. Combine the sauce ingredients in a small bowl.
4. Assemble your cooking tray.

ON YOUR TRAY

Canola oil
Garlic
Bowl of cucumbers
Bowl of snow peas

Bowl of anise
Bowl of sauce
Cornstarch mixture

COOKING

1. Heat a nonstick wok over high heat for 2 minutes.
2. Add 1 teaspoon of the canola oil, then the garlic, and stir-fry for 15 seconds.
3. Add the cucumbers and stir-fry for 2 minutes.
4. Add the snow peas and stir-fry for 1 minute. Remove the vegetables from the wok and set aside.
5. Rinse out the wok, then reheat it for 30 seconds. Pour in the remaining 1 teaspoon of the canola oil, then add the anise and stir-fry for 1 minute.
6. Add the sauce, cover, and reduce the heat to medium. Cook for 2 minutes.
7. Remove the cover, return the cucumbers and snow peas to the wok, and stir.
8. If the sauce seems too thin, add the cornstarch mixture and stir until thickened, about 30 seconds.
9. Remove from the wok, sprinkle with the anise leaves, and serve.

Honey-
Glazed
Brussels
Sprouts
with Red
Pepper

• Brussels sprouts are not a traditional Chinese vegetable, but in this appealing, contemporary recipe they are certainly a welcome addition.

1 pound fresh brussels sprouts, trimmed and cut into halves
1 medium red bell pepper, seeds and ribs removed, and cut into
    1-inch squares

SAUCE

1 cup Vegetable Broth (page 49)
1 tablespoon low-sodium soy sauce
1 tablespoon dry sherry

ADDITIONAL INGREDIENTS

2 teaspoons canola oil
1 tablespoon minced fresh ginger
2 tablespoons honey
1 tablespoon cornstarch dissolved in 2 tablespoons cold water
3 tablespoons finely chopped scallion for garnish

PREPARATION

1. Combine the brussels sprouts and red pepper in a bowl.
2. Combine the sauce ingredients in a small bowl.
3. Assemble your cooking tray.

ON YOUR TRAY

Canola oil   Bowl of sauce
Ginger   Honey
Bowl of brussels sprouts and   Cornstarch mixture
    red pepper

COOKING

1. Heat a nonstick wok over high heat for 2 minutes.
2. Add the canola oil, then the ginger, and stir-fry for 15 seconds.
3. Add the brussels sprouts and red pepper and stir-fry for 1 minute.
4. Pour in the sauce, stir, then cover and reduce the heat to medium-low. Cook for 6 to 7 minutes, or until the brussels sprouts are fork-tender.
5. Remove the cover and raise the heat to high. Stir in the honey, then the cornstarch mixture, and heat until thickened, about 30 seconds.
6. Remove from the wok and sprinkle with the scallions before serving.

Sugar
Snaps and
Shiitakes
in Lemon-
Garlic
Sauce

•

Makes 4
servings

• Sugar snap peas are usually larger and crunchier than snow peas and so add a nice texture to this dish.

4 ounces fresh shiitake mushrooms, stems removed and
     discarded, caps cut into $1/4$-inch slices
12 ounces sugar snap peas, stems and strings removed
$1/2$ cup sliced water chestnuts

SEASONINGS

1 teaspoon minced fresh ginger
1 tablespoon minced fresh garlic

SAUCE

$1/2$ cup Vegetable Broth (page 49) or water
1 tablespoon low-sodium soy sauce
1 tablespoon dry sherry
2 tablespoons lemon juice

ADDITIONAL INGREDIENTS

2 teaspoons canola oil
2 teaspoons cornstarch dissolved in 1 tablespoon cold water

PREPARATION

1. Place the mushrooms, sugar snap peas, and water chestnuts in separate bowls.
2. Combine the seasonings in a small bowl.
3. Combine the sauce ingredients in a small bowl.
4. Assemble your cooking tray.

Canola oil

Bowl of seasonings

Bowl of mushrooms

Bowl of sugar snap peas

Bowl of water chestnuts

Bowl of sauce

Cornstarch mixture

COOKING

1. Heat a nonstick wok over high heat for 2 minutes.
2. Add the canola oil, then the seasonings, and stir-fry for 15 seconds.
3. Add the mushrooms and stir-fry for 1 minute.
4. Add the sugar snap peas and stir-fry for 1 minute.
5. Add the water chestnuts and stir-fry for 30 seconds.
6. Pour in the sauce and stir to combine.
7. If the sauce seems too thin, pour in some of the cornstarch mixture and stir to thicken, about 30 seconds.
8. Remove from the wok and serve.

• Leeks, sweet onions, and scallions all contribute their separate flavors to this Chinese casserole; the coriander adds its distinctive taste, too.

COOKING STOCK

2 leeks
1 teaspoon minced fresh garlic
2 tablespoons minced fresh coriander leaves
2 cups Vegetable Broth (page 49)
2 tablespoons low-sodium soy sauce
1/2 cup dry sherry

ADDITIONAL INGREDIENTS

Canola oil spray
2 teaspoons canola oil
6 large Vidalia or Texas sweet onions, peeled (5 to 6 ounces each)
2 teaspoons cornstarch dissolved in 1 tablespoon cold water
3 scallions, both white and green parts, chopped

PREPARATION

1. Trim the root end of each leek. Cut off and discard the upper green parts, about 2 inches above the white bulbs. Make a cross slit about 1 inch deep in the direction of the bulb end of each leek. Rinse well under cold running water to remove any sand that has lodged in the layers. Coarsely chop the leeks.
2. Combine the ingredients for the stock in a large bowl.
3. Preheat the oven to 400°. Spray a baking dish with canola oil spray.

COOKING

1. Heat a nonstick skillet over high heat for 1 minute.
2. Add the canola oil, then the onions. Brown the onions on all sides. This will take about 5 minutes.
3. Arrange the onions in one layer in the baking dish. Pierce the onions several times with the sharp point of a knife.
4. Pour the cooking stock over the onions and bake uncovered for 30 minutes.
5. Turn the onions and continue baking until the onions are tender, about another 30 minutes.
6. Drain off the cooking liquid into a small saucepan and bring to a boil.
7. Add the cornstarch mixture and stir until thickened. Pour the liquid back over the onions.
8. Sprinkle the onions with the scallions and serve in the baking dish.

• This Chinese version of roasted vegetables can be served cold as a luncheon salad or warm as a vegetable side dish at dinner.

1 anise bulb (fennel)
1 Spanish onion
1 small eggplant (about 1 pound)
1 teaspoon salt

SAUCE

2 tablespoons sesame paste
1 tablespoon low-sodium soy sauce
1 teaspoon chili paste
1 teaspoon sugar
1/4 cup Vegetable Broth (page 49) or water

ADDITIONAL INGREDIENTS

Canola oil spray
2 tablespoons finely chopped anise leaves for garnish

Makes 4
servings

PREPARATION

1. Cut off the long stalks of the anise bulb so only the bulb remains. Cut the bulb into 6 equal wedges.
2. Peel and cut the Spanish onion into 6 equal wedges.
3. Peel and slice the eggplant across into 1/2-inch-thick rounds. Place the rounds on a flat surface and sprinkle with the salt. Set aside for 30 minutes then rinse with cold water, drain, and pat dry with paper towels.
4. Combine the sauce ingredients in a small bowl.
5. Preheat the oven to 450°. Coat two baking sheets with the canola oil spray.

COOKING

1. Arrange the anise and onion wedges in one layer on one of the baking sheets. Spray the vegetables lightly with the canola oil. Bake for 15 minutes, then turn the wedges to brown the other side.
2. Meanwhile, arrange the slices of eggplant on the other baking sheet. Spray the eggplant lightly with the canola oil. Place the eggplant in the oven after the anise and onions have cooked for the first 15 minutes.
3. Roast all the vegetables for 15 minutes more, turning the eggplant slices after 10 minutes.
4. Transfer the vegetables to a large serving bowl.
5. Pour the sauce over the vegetables and mix well.
6. Sprinkle with the anise leaves. Serve warm or at room temperature.

Stir-Fried
Broccoli
and Red
Pepper

•

Makes 4
servings

• 6 to 8 dried Chinese mushrooms, soaked in hot water for 30 minutes
3 cups broccoli florets
1 red bell pepper, seeds and ribs removed, and cut into 1-inch squares

SEASONINGS

1 teaspoon minced fresh ginger
1 teaspoon minced fresh garlic

SAUCE

$^1/_2$ cup Vegetable Broth (page 49) or water
1 tablespoon dry sherry
1 tablespoon low-sodium soy sauce

ADDITIONAL INGREDIENT

2 teaspoons canola oil

PREPARATION

1. Drain the mushrooms from their soaking water and rinse them. Remove and discard the stems. Cut the caps into 1-inch pieces.
2. Place the broccoli in one bowl, and the red pepper and mushrooms in another bowl.
3. Combine the seasonings in a small bowl.
4. Combine the sauce ingredients in a small bowl.
5. Assemble your cooking tray.

ON YOUR TRAY

Canola oil
Bowl of seasonings
Bowl of broccoli

Bowl of red pepper and
   mushrooms
Bowl of sauce

COOKING

1. Heat a nonstick wok over high heat for 2 minutes.
2. Add the canola oil, then the seasonings, and stir-fry for 15 seconds.
3. Add the broccoli and stir-fry for 30 seconds.
4. Add the red pepper and mushrooms and stir-fry for 30 seconds.
5. Pour in the sauce, stir, and reduce the heat to medium. Cover and cook for 3 minutes.
6. Remove the cover and stir. Remove from the wok and serve.

• This Chinese version of pot pie can be served as a luncheon or dinner entrée along with a salad. If you have leftovers, use them in our Curried Vegetable Puffs (pages 28–29).

4 white potatoes, peeled
2 carrots, peeled
2 stalks celery
1 cup broccoli florets
$1/2$ cup frozen peas, thawed
1 teaspoon canola oil
$1/2$ cup chopped onion
1 teaspoon minced fresh ginger
1 teaspoon minced fresh garlic
1 cup Vegetable Broth (page 49)
1 tablespoon low-sodium soy sauce
1 tablespoon curry powder
1 tablespoon cornstarch dissolved in 2 tablespoons cold water
1 (9-inch) unbaked pie pastry, rolled out to cover pie (purchased or see page 29 for Foolproof Pastry Dough)
1 egg white, lightly beaten

PREPARATION

1. Cut the potatoes, carrots, and celery into 1-inch pieces.
2. Bring water to a boil in a saucepan and boil the potatoes for 5 minutes, drain, and set aside in a large bowl.
3. Boil the carrots and celery for 5 minutes, drain, and add to the potatoes.
4. Boil the broccoli florets for 1 minute, drain, and add to the cooked vegetables.
5. Add the thawed green peas to the cooked vegetables. Set aside.

6. Heat the canola oil in a saucepan, add the onion, ginger, and garlic and cook over medium heat until the onions are transparent but not brown.
7. Add the broth, soy sauce, and curry powder and bring to a boil.
8. Add the cornstarch mixture and stir until thickened, about 30 seconds.
9. Combine the broth mixture with the cooked vegetables.
10. Spoon the vegetable mixture into a 9-inch pie plate and cover with the pastry.
11. Brush the top of the pastry with the beaten egg white.

BAKING THE PIE

1. Preheat the oven to 400°.
2. Place the pie on a baking sheet in the center of the oven and bake for 35 to 40 minutes, or until the crust is golden.
3. Remove and let cool for 5 minutes before cutting and serving.

Stir-Fried Asparagus, Golden Peppers, and Water Chestnuts

Makes 4 servings

VEGETABLES

8 ounces fresh asparagus, trimmed and cut into 1-inch pieces
2 yellow bell peppers, seeds and ribs removed, and cut into 1-inch squares
1/2 cup sliced water chestnuts

SEASONINGS

2 teaspoons minced fresh garlic
4 scallions, both white and green parts, chopped

SAUCE

1 cup Vegetable Broth (page 49)
1 tablespoon low-sodium soy sauce
1 tablespoon dry sherry

ADDITIONAL INGREDIENTS

2 teaspoons canola oil
1 tablespoon cornstarch dissolved in 2 tablespoons cold water

PREPARATION

1. Combine the vegetables in a bowl.
2. Combine the seasonings in a small bowl.
3. Combine the sauce ingredients in a bowl.
4. Assemble your cooking tray.

ON YOUR TRAY

Canola oil
Bowl of seasonings
Bowl of vegetables

Bowl of sauce
Cornstarch mixture

COOKING

1. Heat a nonstick wok over high heat for 2 minutes.
2. Add the canola oil, then the seasonings, and stir-fry for 15 seconds.
3. Add the vegetables and stir-fry for 1 minute.
4. Add the sauce, cover, and reduce the heat to medium. Cook for 3 minutes.
5. Remove the cover, return the heat to high. Add the cornstarch mixture and stir until sauce is thickened, about 30 seconds. Serve.

Spaghetti Squash with Spinach

- 1 small spaghetti squash (about 1 ½ pounds)
  1 tablespoon sesame oil
  ½ cup chopped scallions, both white and green parts
  Salt and pepper to taste

SEASONINGS

1 teaspoon minced fresh ginger
1 tablespoon minced fresh garlic
1 teaspoon minced fresh green chili pepper

ADDITIONAL INGREDIENTS

1 teaspoon canola oil
½ cup finely chopped onion
8 ounces fresh spinach, washed and tough stems removed
2 tablespoons pine nuts, lightly toasted over medium heat
    in a dry skillet, for garnish

PREPARATION

1. Preheat the oven to 400°.
2. Cut the squash in half lengthwise and place cut-side down in a baking pan. Pour in 1 inch of water and cover the pan with foil. Bake for 45 minutes.
3. When the squash is cool enough to handle, scoop out the flesh. (It will separate into long, thin, spaghetti-like strands.) Place in a mixing bowl and stir in the sesame oil and scallions. Add salt and pepper to taste.
4. Combine the seasonings in a small bowl.
5. Assemble your cooking tray.

Canola oil
Bowl of seasonings
Bowl of onions

Bowl of spinach
Bowl of spaghetti squash mixture

COOKING

1. Heat a nonstick wok over high heat for 2 minutes.
2. Add the canola oil, then the seasonings, and stir-fry for 15 seconds.
3. Add the onion and stir-fry for 30 seconds.
4. Add the spinach and stir just until wilted, about 30 seconds.
5. Add the spaghetti squash and stir-fry until heated through, about 1 minute.
6. Remove from the wok, sprinkle with the pine nuts, and serve.

Steamed Broccoli and Water Chestnuts in Black Bean Sauce

Makes 4 servings

● SAUCE

1 teaspoon minced fresh garlic
2 tablespoons black bean sauce
2 tablespoons honey
1 tablespoon dry sherry
$^1/_4$ cup Vegetable Broth (page 49) or water

VEGETABLES

4 cups broccoli florets
$^1/_2$ cup sliced water chestnuts

PREPARATION

1. Combine the sauce ingredients in a bowl.
2. Place the broccoli in a heatproof bowl. Sprinkle the water chestnuts over the broccoli and pour the sauce over all.

COOKING

1. Bring 3 to 4 inches of water to a boil in a wok.
2. Place the broccoli mixture in the bowl on a bamboo steamer rack and cover. Place the steamer in the wok over boiling water. Cook for 8 minutes.
3. Remove the steamer from the wok. Wait a minute or two before removing the cover, so you don't burn yourself.
4. Remove the bowl from the steamer and serve.

Desserts
and Tea

RECIPES

- *Fresh Fruit in Cream*

- *Mango Rice Pudding*

- *Almond Cookies*

- *Peach-Berry Almond Tart*

- *Pineapple-Orange Bread Pudding*

- *Star Anise Warm Fruit Compote*

- *Sweet Spiced Almonds*

- *Chinese Tea*

• The Chinese really don't eat sweet desserts, or desserts at all. Sometimes they finish a meal with fresh fruit, so this recipe is our version of a compromise between Chinese practices and Western appetites.

2 ripe bananas, sliced
1 tangerine, separated into sections
1 cup seedless green grapes
6 to 8 dried apricots, coarsely chopped (optional)

CREAM SAUCE

8 ounces soft bean curd
$1/2$ cup vanilla yogurt
1 tablespoon brown sugar
1 teaspoon lemon juice
1 teaspoon tangerine zest
1 teaspoon powdered ginger

ADDITIONAL INGREDIENT

$1/4$ cup sliced almonds, lightly browned in a skillet
over medium heat

1. Place the bananas, tangerines, grapes, and apricots in a large bowl.
2. Combine the cream sauce ingredients in the bowl of a food processor and purée until smooth.
3. Toss the sauce with the fruit and refrigerate until ready to serve.
4. Serve in individual bowls and sprinkle with the almonds.

Mango Rice Pudding

Makes 4 servings

- $^1/_2$ cup rice
- 4 cups skim milk
- $^1/_2$ teaspoon cinnamon
- 1 ripe mango, peeled and pitted, and cut into $^1/_2$-inch pieces
- $^1/_4$ cup plum sauce
- 2 eggs, lightly beaten

1. Combine the rice and milk in a saucepan and bring to a boil. Reduce the heat to low and simmer for 45 minutes, stirring from time to time.
2. Add the cinnamon, mango, and plum sauce to the rice mixture and cook another 10 minutes.
3. Remove a small amount of the hot pudding and stir it into the beaten eggs.
4. Return the egg mixture to the pudding and stir constantly until it thickens, 2 to 3 minutes.
5. Transfer the pudding to a bowl and cool slightly. Refrigerate until ready to serve. It will thicken more as it chills.

• We think these almond cookies will be a revelation to you. Almond cookies usually are hard and dry, but these will melt in your mouth—it's the cornstarch that makes the difference.

Almond Cookies

•

Makes 2 dozen

1 cup vegetable shortening or butter
1 cup granulated sugar
1 egg
2 tablespoons pure almond extract
1 $^1/_2$ cups flour
1 cup cornstarch
2 teaspoons baking soda
$^1/_2$ teaspoon salt
24 whole almonds, blanched

1. Preheat the oven to 350°. Grease a baking sheet.
2. Combine the shortening and sugar in a mixing bowl and beat until creamy.
3. Add the egg and beat until well blended.
4. Stir in the almond extract.
5. In a separate bowl, sift together the flour, cornstarch, baking soda, and salt.
6. Combine the shortening mixture with the flour mixture. It will be a stiff dough.
7. Roll the dough into 1-inch balls and place at least 2 inches apart on the baking sheet.
8. Flatten the cookies slightly and place an almond in the center of each one, pressing down so the dough cracks slightly around the nut.
9. Place the baking sheet in the center of the oven and bake for 10 to 12 minutes, or until the bottoms are lightly browned but the tops are still pale.
10. Cool on a rack. The cookies will keep for up to two weeks stored in an airtight container.

Peach-Berry Almond Tart

Makes 6 to 8 servings

• This tart is best made when peaches and strawberries are in season. When the fruit is fresh and ripe, it cooks up to a soft consistency and has extra flavor that contrasts nicely with the taste of the almonds.

6 fresh peaches, peeled and cut into 1-inch chunks (4 cups)
2 cups fresh strawberries, rinsed (cut larger berries in half)
1/2 cup granulated sugar
3 tablespoons cornstarch
1 cup frozen peach juice concentrate
1/4 cup lemon juice
1 teaspoon almond extract
1 Pastry Crust (recipe follows)
1/4 cup sliced almonds, lightly toasted in a dry skillet
     over medium heat

1. Combine the peaches and strawberries in a large bowl and set aside.
2. Combine the sugar and cornstarch in a saucepan and mix well.
3. Add the peach juice concentrate and bring to a boil, stirring constantly.
4. Boil until the mixture thickens, about 1 minute.
5. Remove the pan from the heat and stir in the lemon juice and almond extract. Cool for 10 minutes, stirring occasionally.
6. Drain the fruit, then combine with the sauce.
7. Spoon the fruit mixture into the prebaked pastry crust and sprinkle the almonds over the top.

PASTRY CRUST
Makes 1 crust

$^1/_4$ cup shortening
$^1/_4$ cup granulated sugar
1 egg yolk
1 cup flour
$^1/_2$ cup finely ground almonds

1. Preheat the oven to 350°.
2. Combine the shortening and sugar and beat until creamy.
3. Add the egg yolk and mix well.
4. Combine the flour and ground almonds, then add to the sugar mixture. Using a pastry blender or food processor, combine until the mixture resembles fine bread crumbs.
5. Press the pastry mixture into a 9-inch pie or tart pan.
6. Bake for 10 to 12 minutes, or until the edges are lightly browned. Cool before filling the crust.

*Pineapple-
Orange
Bread
Pudding*

•

*Makes 6
servings*

- Canola oil spray
  3 eggs, lightly beaten
  1 (12-ounce) can evaporated skim milk plus enough water to make 3 cups
  $^1\!/_4$ cup sugar
  $^1\!/_2$ teaspoon ground ginger
  $^1\!/_2$ teaspoon ground cinnamon, plus some for garnish
  4 to 6 (1-inch-thick) slices day-old French bread
  $^1\!/_2$ cup orange marmalade
  $^1\!/_2$ fresh ripe pineapple, peeled, cored, and cut into 1-inch cubes

1. Preheat the oven to 325°. Spray a 2-quart baking dish with the canola oil spray.
2. Combine the eggs, milk mixture, sugar, ginger, and $^1\!/_2$ teaspoon cinnamon in a bowl and mix well with a whisk.
3. Spread the bread slices with the marmalade and cut into 1-inch cubes.
4. Mix the bread and pineapple cubes in the baking dish.
5. Pour the egg mixture over the bread mixture and set aside for 30 minutes.
6. Sprinkle the top with a dusting of cinnamon.
7. Bake for 45 minutes, or until golden.

• Star anise contributes a delicate licorice flavor to this warm fruit compote.

1 1/2 cups water
1/4 cup lemon juice
1/2 cup apricot jam
1 tablespoon crumbled star anise
1 cinnamon stick, or 1/2 teaspoon ground cinnamon
2 apples, peeled, cored, and cut into 1/4-inch slices
2 pears, peeled, cored, and cut into 1/4-inch slices
1/2 cup dried apricots, cut in half
1 cup seedless red grapes
Zest of 1 lemon

1. Combine the water, lemon juice, apricot jam, star anise, and cinnamon in a large saucepan and bring to a boil.
2. Lower the heat and simmer for 15 minutes.
3. Strain the apricot jam mixture to remove the star anise and cinnamon stick, then return the mixture to the stove.
4. Add the apples, pears, and apricots and simmer for 5 minutes.
5. Remove from the heat and stir in the red grapes.
6. Transfer to a glass bowl and garnish with the lemon zest. Serve warm.

*Star Anise
Warm
Fruit
Compote*

•

*Makes 4
servings*

Sweet Spiced Almonds

Makes about 3 ¹/₂ cups

• The Chinese love their snacks. Here is an easy-to-make sweet almond concoction.

Canola oil spray

SPICES

1 teaspoon ground cinnamon
1 teaspoon ground ginger
¹/₄ cup granulated sugar

ADDITIONAL INGREDIENTS

1 pound unsalted whole almonds, blanched
1 egg white lightly beaten with 2 tablespoons cold water

1. Preheat the oven to 225°. Coat a baking sheet with the canola oil spray.
2. Combine the spices in a small bowl.
3. Combine the almonds with the egg white mixture. Then toss the almonds with the spice mixture.
4. Spread the almonds on the baking sheet and bake for 50 to 60 minutes, stirring every 15 minutes.
5. Store in an airtight container. Serve as a snack, or as a sweet at the end of a meal.

• The tea usually served in Chinese restaurants is black tea, which is fermented. The Chinese, however, favor green tea, which has the most delicate flavor of the Chinese teas. The plant's tender, young, top leaves are specially selected for green tea and are not fermented. The best green teas can be prized and priced like fine wines. Some Chinese teas add flower or fruit blossoms for a distinctive flowery taste. Jasmine tea is an example of this.

The Chinese might or might not have tea with their meals, but the best teas are saved for after dinner or special occasions. Or they are sipped at home or in a tea house at nonmeal times when their special flavors can be savored on their own.

A minimal selection of Chinese teas usually is available in a supermarket. But to find good-quality green teas, you will have to go to a Chinese market. The prices of the teas will vary with their quality. Try several different ones to compare the tastes and see which you prefer.

Here is the way we brew tea to best bring out its flavor.

Makes 6 to 8 cups of tea

6 cups water
3 teaspoons loose tea

1. Warm your teapot first by filling it with boiling water and setting it aside 2 to 3 minutes before brewing the tea. This will help to keep the tea hot longer.
2. Bring the water to a rapid boil in a saucepan.
3. Empty out the water that has been warming the teapot. Place the loose tea in the teapot.
4. Pour one inch of the boiling water over the tea leaves, cover, and allow the tea to steep for 3 minutes.
5. Add the remainder of the boiling water and serve.

The following list describes the special Chinese ingredients we use in this book. Most of them can be found in well-stocked supermarkets or in vegetable markets or health food stores.

Baby Corn These miniature ears of corn are available canned in most supermarkets and health food stores.

Bean Curd Made from soybeans, water, and a curdling agent, bean curd is an important source of protein in a vegetarian diet and an integral part of Chinese cuisine. Also known as tofu, it comes in several varieties but the two used in this book are soft and firm fresh bean curd cakes. Soft bean curd has more liquid and a more custardlike consistency than the firm version. These varieties of bean curd are available in the produce departments of most supermarkets and health food stores. You can store bean curd in water in a covered container in the refrigerator. If you change the water every day or two, it will keep for up to two weeks. Bean curd has almost no taste on its own, but it easily takes on the flavors of other ingredients it is cooked with.

Bean Sprouts Fresh bean sprouts are carried in the produce departments of most grocery stores. Mung bean sprouts are smaller and are more delicate than soy bean sprouts. Keep bean sprouts fresh by washing them in cold water, and then storing them in water in a covered container in the refrigerator. If you change the water every couple of days, they should keep for a week.

Black Bean Sauce This salty, fermented bean sauce is a very popular Chinese flavoring. The beans can be found in sauce form in cans or jars, often with garlic added. Most supermarkets and well-stocked food stores carry black bean sauce. Refrigerate the jar after opening.

Bok Choy This distinctive Chinese cabbage has milky white stalks and deep green leaves. It is easily found in the produce department of most grocery stores.

Cellophane Noodles These thin spaghetti-like noodles are made from mung beans rather than wheat flour. They become transparent when cooked and have an almost gelatin-like consistency. We use them in soups and salads. Cellophane noodles can be found in Asian markets and some health food stores and supermarkets. They are sold dried, in small plastic-wrapped packages, sometimes labeled "bean threads" or "Chinese vermicelli."

Chili Paste This spicy sauce, which is frequently used in Szechuan recipes, is made from hot chili peppers. You can find it in jars in the Asian food section of well-stocked supermarkets.

Chili Peppers Green chili peppers, also known as jalpeño peppers, are sold fresh in the produce department of most grocery stores. Dried red chili peppers also are sold in produce departments. Frequently used as a flavoring in Szechuan and Hunan dishes, dried red chili peppers are extremely hot. Don't eat the peppers themselves; remove and discard them before the food is served.

Chinese Egg Noodles These fresh flour and egg noodles are much better than dried noodles in lo mein dishes and other Chinese noodle recipes. Look for these noodles, or their Japanese or American or Italian counterparts, wherever you find fresh pasta in the supermarket.

Chinese Hot Oil This hot pepper oil is used in very small quantities in some spicy dishes. You can substitute Tabasco or another hot red pepper sauce.

Chinese Mustard Available in powder form or in bottles in the Asian food section of most supermarkets, Chinese mustard is extremely hot. Use it sparingly. To make mustard from the dried powder, mix it with equal parts water or rice vinegar.

Coriander We frequently use this herb in our recipes. Often labeled cilantro in the market, fresh coriander has a very identifiable taste. It is also called Chinese parsley.

Dried Chinese Mushrooms These large, flat, dried mushrooms have a delicate flavor and a chewy consistency when cooked. If you can't find the Chinese version, get the Japanese equivalent, shiitake mushrooms, which are available in most supermarkets. Dried mushrooms should be cleaned thoroughly and soaked for 30 minutes in hot water before using. The stems should be cut off; only the cap is used.

Duck Sauce We use this sweet, chutneylike sauce for a dipping sauce with some of our recipes. Also known as plum sauce, duck sauce is sold in jars in the Asian food section of most supermarkets.

Dumpling Wrappers These small, round dough skins are sold in packages in the refrigerated cases of Asian markets and in some well-stocked supermarkets. Wonton wrappers are made of the same dough, but they are square; dumpling wrappers are round. With a little manipulation, either one may be used in most recipes. Once the package is opened, wrap the remaining wrappers carefully in plastic wrap so they won't dry out. They will keep for a week or so in the refrigerator or for months in the freezer.

Five-Spice Powder This popular Chinese spice mixture combines ginger, cloves, anise, fennel, and cinnamon. You can mix these five spices together in equal quantities from your own spice collection if you can't find it in your market.

Garlic You may be surprised at how frequently garlic is used as a seasoning in Chinese recipes. Fresh minced garlic is preferred, but the bottled minced version that has become popular in stores can be substituted.

Ginger One of the primary Chinese flavorings, ginger is used in a great number of recipes. You can find this knobby, brown root in the produce department of most grocery stores. It also is sold minced in jars. The jarred version is easier to keep and is all right to use in most of our recipes, except for the ones that call for sliced, not minced, ginger. Fresh ginger roots should be washed, peeled, and minced before using. Store the jarred minced ginger and fresh ginger root in the refrigerator. To make fresh ginger last longer, place it in sherry in a covered container. Ginger also may be frozen. It's easier to use later if you freeze it in tablespoon-sized pieces.

Please note that powdered ginger has a very different flavor from ginger root and is not a substitute for it.

Hoisin Sauce This sweet and pungent sauce, made from soy beans and Chinese herbs and spices, is another popular Chinese flavoring. You can buy it in jars in the Asian food section of most supermarkets. Store the jar in the refrigerator after opening.

Pine Nuts These small, light-colored nuts are sometimes called by their Italian name *pignoli*. We use them in a number of recipes instead of peanuts.

Plum Sauce See Duck Sauce.

Rice Noodles Rice noodles are available either fresh, in sheets (which you will have to cut yourself) or dry, as packaged, thin vermicelli-like noodles called rice sticks. Rice noodles have a distinctive, delicate taste, and are sold in Asian markets. If you can't find them, substitute a thin spaghetti or vermicelli.

Rice Vinegar Chinese rice vinegar or the similar Japanese rice vinegar are available in most supermarkets. Rice vinegar has a softer, less acid taste than cider vinegar, which is more commonly used in the U.S.

Sesame Oil Chinese sesame oil has a much richer, nuttier taste than Western sesame oils. Be sure to use a Chinese or Japanese brand of sesame oil in your Chinese recipes. You can find one in most supermarkets.

Sesame Paste This paste is made from roasted sesame seeds and soy beans. The nutty flavor of sesame seeds is the predominant taste. It is sold in jars and should be refrigerated when opened. Look for sesame paste in the Asian food section of your supermarket or in an Asian market.

Soy Sauce This most popular Chinese seasoning is, unfortunately, high in sodium, so we recommend using a low-sodium version. Check the nutrition counts on the labels. Because of the still-high sodium counts in even the lowest-sodium soy sauce, we generally use less of it than normally would be used in Chinese recipes.

Spring Roll Wrappers These wrappers are more delicate than egg roll wrappers but are not as easy to find. In an Asian market, they are located in the refrigerated cases. If you don't have an Asian market nearby, use egg roll wrappers, which many supermarkets do carry.

Star Anise When whole, this spice has the shape of a star—hence its name. It has a distinctive licorice taste. Star anise is sold in small packages in Asian markets and some well-stocked supermarkets. The powdered anise found in the supermarket spice department has a bland flavor; but if that is all you can find, use it.

Straw Mushrooms These small, umbrella-shaped, tan mushrooms are used in a lot of Chinese recipes for their elegant look and delicate flavor. Canned straw mushrooms are available in most markets; some carry dried straw mushrooms. The dried ones need to be soaked in hot water for 30 minutes before using to soften them up.

Water Chestnuts This is not really a nut but the bulb of a plant than grows in water. And since it is not a nut, water chestnuts—like most vegetables—have almost no fat. With a delicate flavor, a nice crunchy texture, and no fat, no wonder the water chestnut is a popular Chinese ingredient. It is easy to find in cans but is sometimes available fresh in the produce departments of supermarkets. Canned water chestnuts will do, but fresh ones are preferred for their more distinctive taste. Fresh water chestnuts need to be washed, peeled, and sliced thinly before using. Fresh or canned water chestnuts will last for a couple of weeks if you keep them in water in a closed container in the refrigerator. Be sure to change the water every couple of days.

Wonton Wrappers See Dumpling wrappers.

Green chili pepper
Curried Corn and Red Pepper Salad,
56–57
defined, 162
Eggplant Dip, 14–15
Hoisin Noodles with Vegetables,
106–108
Sesame Noodles with Cucumbers and
Red Radishes, 96–97
Spaghetti Squash with Spinach,
146–147
Spinach-Stuffed Mushrooms, 16–17
Steamed Squash Rolls, 22–23
Sweet Potato–Green Chili Soup, 39
Tangerines and Snow Peas
on Picks, 13
Vegetarian Spring Rolls, 24–27
Green peas
Cauliflower Soup with Carrots and
Peas, 38
Curried Vegetable Pie, 142–143
Steamed Vegetables with Watercress
and Coriander Sauce, 112–113
Grilled Dragon Kabobs, 18

H

Hoisin Green Beans and Peppers,
116–117
Hoisin Noodles with Vegetables,
106–108
Hoisin sauce, defined, 164
Honey-Glazed Brussels Sprouts with Red
Pepper, 132–133
Horseradish Dipping Sauce, 20–21
Hot and Sour Vegetable Soup, 36–37

Hot and Sour Vegetables, 114–115
Hot oil, defined, 162
Hot Pepper Rice Sticks with Peanuts,
102–103

K

Kiwifruits, and spinach salad, 58

L

Leeks
Glazed Sweet and Sour Leeks,
126–127
Golden Squash Soup with Leeks, 40–41
Hot and Sour Vegetable Soup, 36–37
Seared Bean Curd with Sesame-Ginger
Sauce, 68–69
Spinach Fried Brown Rice, 90–91
Steamed Vegetables with Watercress
and Coriander Sauce, 112–113
Triple Onion Bake, 136–137
Lima bean, and velvet corn soup, 45
Low-sodium soy sauce, 164

M

Mandarin orange, and cucumber
salad, 60
Mango
rice pudding, 152
salad with creamy cucumber dressing, 61
Minted Fruit Salad, 62–63
Melon
Chilled Pineapple-Melon Soup, 47
Minted Fruit Salad, 62–63
Minted Fruit Salad, 62–63

S